D1570456

THE BEST KEPT KEPT SECRET ON WALL STREET

How To Invest in
Convertible
Securities
Like the Pros

WAYNE F. NELSON

Dearborn
Financial Publishing, Inc.

While a great deal of care has been taken to provide accurate and current information, the ideas, suggestions, general principles and conclusions presented in this text are subject to local, state and federal laws and regulations, court cases and any revisions of same. The reader is thus urged to consult legal counsel regarding any points of law—this publication should not be used as a substitute for competent legal advice.

Publisher: Kathleen A. Welton
Associate Editor: Karen A. Christensen
Editorial Assistant: Kristen G. Landreth
Senior Project Editor: Jack L. Kiburz
Interior Design: Lucy Jenkins
Cover Design: Michael S. Finkelman, Shot in the Dark Design

Published by Dearborn Financial Publishing, Inc.

Printed in the United States of America

93 94 95 10 9 8 7 6 5 4 3 2 1

Library of Congress Cataloging-in-Publication Data

Nelson, Wayne F.
    The best kept secret on Wall Street : how to invest in convertible securities like the pros / by Wayne F. Nelson
        p. cm.
    Includes index.
    ISBN 0-79310-720-2
    1. Convertible securities. I. Title.
HG4651.N34   1993
332.63′2044—dc20   93-21502
                                                            CIP

DEDICATION

For Marti, my best buddy

ACKNOWLEDGMENTS

If this book were a child, he or she would be old enough for grade school. I started this project in 1986. My lovely wife, Marti, and every one of my clients are by now weary of hearing about "the convertible securities book." Half of the convertibles that existed when I began writing have been called or converted. The convertible marketplace has changed, from one influenced principally by small companies, to junk financings, to zero coupons, to large companies and now back to small companies. I have watched the performance of convertibles throughout the fantastic voyage of the Dow Jones industrial average to and through 3,600, the crash of 1987, the correction of 1989, the war over Kuwait and a couple of Presidential elections. As a result, I have learned a great deal about convertible securities—all of which is included in this book.

Thanks to everyone who provided assistance with this book. At the top of the list are my staff members, Laura McArtor, Nancy Skonberg, Maggie Shriver, Michael Kirvan and Francis Kalitsi, who have been extraordinarily supportive and have made countless valuable contributions. These talented people did all the behind-the-scenes work. They tracked down hard-to-find data, did the research and involved themselves completely in the overall project. I am especially grateful to Laura McArtor, whose word processing and editing skills brought this project to completion ahead of deadline. In Washington, that is a very big deal. Haley Kaufman prepared the entire mutual fund chapter. That took a considerable amount of time and effort, which is greatly appreciated. John Yount, a former apprentice, is largely responsible for this book's glossary. Nancy Skonberg wrote an entire chapter about fundamental security analysis which, in the end, we decided did not fit well in this book. Her effort is no less sincerely appreciated.

Launny Steffens, who runs the private client group for Merrill Lynch; Preston Harrington and Bernie Moriarty, convertible analysts for Merrill Lynch; and Bruce Chappel, a Merrill colleague in the Jacksonville, Florida office, were all extraordinarily helpful with their suggestions and information.

Ed Mathias, managing director of T. Rowe Price; Andy Brooks, manager of the trading department of T. Rowe Price; Mark Hunt, managing director of convertible securities for Smith Barney; and Tom Madden and Greg Melvin, portfolio managers for the Federated Mutual Funds family also provided a considerable amount of helpful information.

Most important of all, I am grateful for the encouragement of my best friend and lovely wife, Marti. To all who have so patiently helped me with this project, here it is at last, "the convertible book."

DISCLAIMER

The opinions, views and thoughts set forth in this book are solely those of Wayne F. Nelson and have not been approved or endorsed by any other person, including, but not limited to, the author's present or past employers.

CONTENTS

PREFACE

Convertibles work! Just understanding that they exist, how they can work for you and when they work best can put you at an advantage as an investor. There are plenty of smart people who don't enjoy that edge—because they don't understand what you will when you finish this book. A slight edge in the world of investing can mean a difference in lifestyle. With that in mind, let me help you uncover the best-kept secret on Wall Street.

The title of this book, *The Best Kept Secret on Wall Street,* is not intended to suggest that convertible securities are a get-rich-quick scheme that only a few so far have discovered. This title was chosen to emphasize the point that too few investors have made the effort to learn about these fascinating financial instruments. In certain instances, a convertible security can be the most appropriate way to invest in a particular company. We want you to be able to recognize those opportunities.

Convertibles, which come in two forms—bonds and preferred stock—usually offer a higher yield than the investment into which they can be converted (exchanged). And they offer the potential for appreciation if what they can be exchanged into increases in value. They are defensive investments because of these higher yields; that is, their higher yields cause them to trade more like bonds than stocks. Because convertibles are not as volatile as common stocks, they often give an investor fair warning to make changes. For this reason, they can be a more conservative way to participate in the market. Yet, because they participate in the market, they offer growth potential that an investor cannot get in a "straight" or traditional fixed-income investment. For example, money market funds, Treasury bills and savings certificates pay a fixed rate of return but provide no opportunity for growth of the money invested in them.

Convertible securities also pay a fixed rate of return, but because their value is linked to an investment that can gain or lose value, the link provides potential for gain or loss. Also as a result, convertibles act a little differently from stocks or bonds. They are multifaceted investments. This characteristic causes many investors to shun the convertible market entirely. Rather than make the effort to understand how the market works, many investors choose to use something that seems less complicated. Herein lies the best-kept secret on Wall Street. If you make the effort, you will become one of a relatively small number of individual investors who can knowledgeably buy, sell and manage convertible securities as part of their investment portfolio. And you will be rewarded for that effort.

One of the most appealing aspects of the convertible marketplace, as large as it has become, is that there are still market inefficiencies. And inefficiencies result in bargains for investors knowledgeable enough to spot them. This is why inefficiencies in the convertible market exist.

Institutional investors generally favor very sizable convertible issues that are easy to buy and sell in large dollar amounts. Of the approximately 750 existing issues, perhaps only one-third meet that criterion. That leaves plenty of opportunity for the rest of us to trade issues that may be all but ignored by professional investors. There is a strong likelihood that you will be able to find mispricing among issues that are not of institutional interest. A knowledgeable individual investor has an advantage in this marketplace that he or she enjoys in few others. That is part of the excitement of convertible investing.

And there are plenty of other reasons to invest in convertibles. For risk-averse investors who might not otherwise commit serious money to common stocks, a convertible offers an alternative to a full-blown retreat from equity investing. For yield-sensitive investors who are not satisfied with low money market returns, convertible securities on average pay double today's money market rates. The fixed return can be a soothing feature in uncertain times. For investors who recognize that some of their assets should be committed to investments with growth potential, convertibles offer a way to add balance to their portfolios.

CHAPTER 1

What Convertibles Are and Why They May Be the Most Attractive Way To Invest in a Company

Convertible securities can be very attractive investments. They generally pay a higher return than common stocks and involve less risk. Over the past ten years, results of convertible investing include a total return of over 500 percent, with no down years! *In half of those years convertibles outperformed common stocks, and in seven of the ten they outperformed straight (nonconvertible) bonds.* (See Figure 1.1.) Counting appreciation and income, the typical convertible has a total return over three times greater than that of the average fixed-income security. (See Figure 1.2.) Convertibles have also been less volatile than nonconvertible securities. During the two most recent violent market corrections, convertibles held up much better than common stocks. On October 19, 1987, according to Lipper Analytical Service, convertible funds fell 16.12 percent versus 22.53 percent for the Standard & Poor's 500 stock average. And on October 13, 1989, according to a Smith Barney study, while the stock market dropped approximately 7 percent that day, the average convertible fell only 2.53 percent or, only 49 percent as much as the underlying common stock.

Yet, despite an impressive long-term performance record, convertible securities remain Wall Street's orphans. They are unloved, neglected and too frequently misunderstood.

FIGURE 1.1   Convertible Performance versus Common Stocks

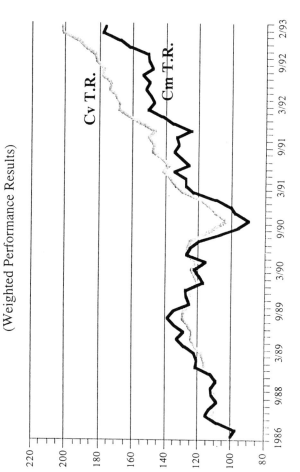

Smith Barney 400: Convertible Index
(Weighted Performance Results)

Source: Reprinted by permission of Smith Barney.

FIGURE 1.2 Convertible Performance versus the Long Bond

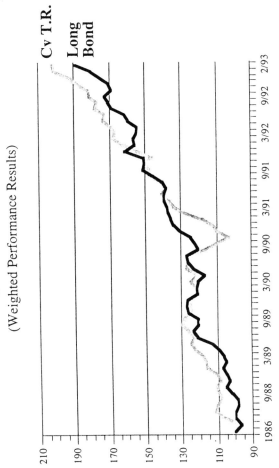

Smith Barney 400: Convertible Index

(Weighted Performance Results)

Source: Reprinted by permission of Smith Barney.

The reason is that convertibles are perceived to be complicated investments appropriate only for the most sophisticated investor. But that just is not the case. There is a role for convertible securities in nearly every investor's portfolio. The goal of this book is to help you determine where convertibles could work best for you. We want you to understand what convertible securities are, how they work and when to use them. We want you to train yourself to ask, when you consider an investment, whether a convertible exists and then to be able to quickly determine whether that convertible is the smartest way to invest in the company.

Beyond that, this book will show you where to get good convertible investment ideas. It will help you evaluate the potential risks and rewards of such investments. We want you to recognize the difference between bargains and land mines. It will help you make better sell-or-convert decisions. It will not only help you understand where convertibles fit into your overall investment program but also teach you how to work with your investment adviser to get good overall investment results.

Convertibles have been called the "quintessential investment for fence sitters." That's silly. It implies that if you can't decide whether to own the stock or the bond of a company you like, you do neither (or both, depending on your vantage point) by selecting the convertible. Smart investing is often a matter of timing. You may be in love with a company for all the right reasons and be absolutely correct about its merits as a good long-term investment. Eventually, the company's stock may reward you. No one but God knows when that will be (and as the ultimate insider, He is not saying). Getting paid well while you wait can certainly make the wait more tolerable.

CONVERTIBLE SECURITIES DEFINED

A *convertible security* is a bond or preferred stock that can be exchanged, or converted, at the holder's option into common stock. The allure of a convertible is its split personality: it combines the safety and income feature of a bond with the appreciation potential of a stock. Like a bond, a convertible pays a fixed rate of interest that is almost always higher than the dividend from the company's common stock. Like a common stock, a convertible can appreciate in value with the good fortunes of the company, because a convertible can be exchanged at the investor's option for the company's stock. In fact, this is the major reason for owning convertibles: *As the price of the underlying common stock rises, so should the price of the convertible.* Furthermore, convertibles are by definition *senior securities,* giving their owners preferential treatment over common stock owners in the event of financial distress on the part of the issuing company. The higher quality and almost always higher income support the convertible's price, should the common stock fall.

A HISTORICAL PERSPECTIVE OF CONVERTIBLES

Convertible securities are not a new phenomenon but have a long history as investments. In the early 1600s, King Charles I of England owned stock in the London Water Company that was convertible into bonds. Convertibles played a major role in building railroads in U.S. history. Jay Gould, Daniel Drew and Cornelius Vanderbilt financed their railroad empires by issuing convertible bonds. In the early 1900s, AT&T, Lackawanna Steel, Otis Elevator and Diamond Match used convertibles to raise money. In the 1960s, convertibles were widely used to finance the corporate entity of that decade: the conglomerate—that is, holding companies consisting of many companies unrelated to one another. Among those conglomerates were W. R. Grace, Gulf & Western, ITT and Ling-Tempo-Vought. The 1970s was a quiet period for convertibles, as it was a slow time for common stocks. That changed with the beginning of the bull market in August 1982 when many new convertible issues came to market, the majority of them offered by small-technology growth companies. (See Figure 1.3.) In 1989 there were 67 new convertible issues, whereas in 1974 there were only 8. In 1984 IBM added respectability to the convertible market, which at the time primarily consisted of issues from smaller, less-well-known companies, by issuing a $1.5 billion convertible bond to finance its purchase of Rolm Corporation. In the 1980s as well, many corporations and corporate raiders used convertibles to finance mergers, acquisitions and buyouts. Some of those convertibles were referred to as *junk bonds*.

Historically, convertibles have been issued by smaller growth companies, by companies with a lot of debt and by companies that have come into being as a result of a merger or spinoff. That has changed. Such major corporations as du Pont, Walt Disney, Litton, Motorola, WMX Technology and Services (formerly Waste Management), Pfizer, Marriott and MCI have been convertible issuers. More of these high-quality issues are coming to the market every month as the size of the convertible market mushrooms. Based on the *value* of all the convertibles in the market today, major corporation offerings now account for more than half of the total. That is a significant change. In the past, the convertible securities marketplace had always been regarded as a backwater investment field dominated by smaller, lesser-quality companies. (See Figure 1.4.)

Based on the number of issues, however, those smaller companies still account for roughly two-thirds of the marketplace. Yet one-third of the Standard & Poor's 500 companies now have a convertible security in the market—and that number is growing. *The convertible marketplace today is more attractive than it has ever been, as convertible securities are being offered by more high-quality companies than ever before. Add to this the fact that today's convertibles as a group yield three times more than common stocks and nearly as much as nonconvertible bonds, and you can understand their investment appeal.*

WHY COMPANIES ISSUE CONVERTIBLE SECURITIES

Smaller growth companies issue convertible bonds rather than straight bonds or common stock, because people who have traditionally invested in those kinds of companies have demanded more than interest payments for their investments. Investors often want a share

FIGURE 1.3 New Issues of Convertibles

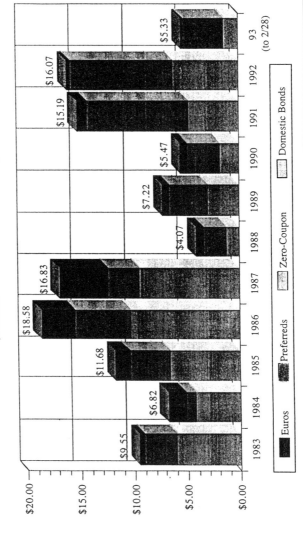

New Convertible Issue Volume
(Market Value at Time of Issue)

FIGURE 1.4 Convertible Securities Marketplace

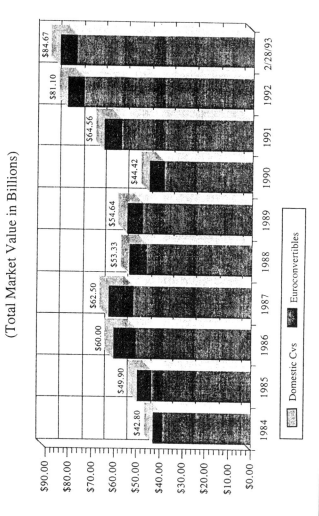

Total Size of Convertible Market
(Total Market Value in Billions)

Source: Reprinted by permission of Smith Barney.

of the company's growth potential as well as interest payments. They believe that because the risk is higher investing in smaller growth companies, they should be compensated accordingly. The insistence on an equity stake, or *kicker,* is similar to what a venture capital firm gets when it helps to finance a company in its earliest developmental stages. In return for cash that the company desperately needs, a venture capital firm usually receives a significant ownership interest in the company. Giving up some of their equity is frequently the only way for these companies to raise money. Smaller corporations that issue convertibles to raise money are further along in their growth pattern than those financed by venture capitalists, but they are fragile enough so that *investors* have more to say about the terms of the investment. Since those terms frequently call for a piece of the company, convertible securities are commonly used. When a company reaches the lofty status of a Litton, Disney or du Pont, on the other hand, the *company* is in a position to dictate how it will accept investors.

Large companies issue convertibles when they view them as the cheapest way to raise capital. That happens when the interest rate they would pay to borrow money by selling a convertible is meaningfully lower than what they would pay by issuing a straight or nonconvertible issue. Another reason large companies issue convertible bonds is that convertible bond interest payments are often cheaper than dividend payments made by a company on its common stock—cheaper because interest payments are a *tax-deductible expense* for a corporation, while dividend payments are not.

Interest payments are considered an expense item for a corporation. They are paid before the company's profit is calculated and before taxes are paid on that profit. Dividends are paid after taxes and out of the company's profits. It is often cheaper for a corporation to pay interest on a bond (convertibles included) than to pay dividends on common stock shares. Think of interest payments for a corporation as being tax deductible, while common stock dividends are not.

Corporations are also more likely to issue convertible securities when the price of their common stock is high. A company's management is well aware when the price of the company's stock represents its full value. When it does, it makes all the sense in the world, from management's point of view, to raise money by selling more common shares. A convertible offering not only accomplishes that purpose but it does one thing more. A convertible offering is a sale of the shares at a *premium,* or markup, to the current common share price. That is because convertibles are usually issued so that the underlying common share price needs to go up from 12 percent to 20 percent to make the conversion take place. Because nearly 85 percent of all convertible issues eventually become common shares, the company regards a convertible offering as a future, higher-price common share offering. And, as we learned earlier about the lower interest expense a corporation incurs by issuing a convertible, the cost of carrying this advanced higher-share-price offering is, for the corporation, cheaper than issuing common stock and paying a dividend on those additional common shares now.

This is how it works. Let's say the corporation's common stock is trading at $35 a share, the common stock pays a $2-per-share dividend and the company wants to raise $100 million. Let's further assume that the company can sell a convertible security with a 15 percent *conversion premium* (more about this term later). For now, think of this transaction from management's standpoint. A 15 percent conversion premium is equal to 15 percent above the current market price of the company's common stock. So, rather than selling shares at $35 each (the current market price of the common), offering a convertible at a 15 percent premium has the same effect as selling shares at $40.25 each:

$$\$35 \times 15\% = \$5.25, \$35 + 5.25 = \$40.25$$

The $100 million raised by selling the convertible will eventually become $115 million of common stock. In the meantime, the cost of the offering at a 7½ percent interest rate is approximately $4.5 million after tax:

$$\$100 \text{ million debt} \times 7\tfrac{1}{2}\% = \$7.5 \text{ million} \times 40\% \text{ tax rate} =$$
$$\$3.0 \text{ million tax deduction} = \$4.5 \text{ million}$$

Had the company sold common, it would have had to sell it at the current market price and pay $5.7 million in dividends. Remember, the common dividend is $2 a share a year. Its cost of money in that case would have been $2.2 million more:

$100 million offering = 285,714 new shares × $2 per share
dividend = $5.7 million

$5.7 million dividend payment – $4.5 million net
convertible payment = $2.2 million.

WHY INVESTORS BUY CONVERTIBLES

In May 1988 I was chatting with my neighbor, a fellow who works for MCI Corporation, the long-distance telephone company. When I told him I was writing a magazine article about local company stocks, he told me, "Be sure to include MCI." Oh sure, I thought, nodding skeptically. MCI's stock had been trading at $6 a share for as long as I could remember. Having dropped from the high $30s, it had been given up by investors. At that time MCI was one of those stocks we ungraciously refer to as "dogs." But my neighbor persisted in his praise of the company as a great turnaround and told me about the significant new business the company was booking almost daily. Curious, I arranged to visit Bill McGowan, MCI's late chairman, to talk about his company for the article. After that visit, I, too, was convinced about the prospects of the company and began recommending MCI stock.

Many of my clients are risk-averse investors who don't like a stock that doesn't pay a dividend. And at $6 a share, MCI seemed like a pretty speculative investment. Because MCI had been trading around the same price for some time, it did not appear to many investors to be going anywhere soon. To those people, I suggested the MCI convertible bond. These $1,000 face value bonds were trading at about $940 at that time. At that price they yielded 8.25 percent, which was nearly as high as the return from money market funds at that time (as hard as that is to believe now). Take the money out of the money market fund and buy the MCI converts; you'll earn the same interest, I told them, and if we are right and the stock goes up, the bonds will go up in value as well. Give your money some chance to grow.

It worked out. The company did as well as my neighbor and Bill McGowan had predicted. MCI common stock moved from $6 to the high $30s before the convertible bonds were called at $1,035 each by the company. In seven months, those investors made $95 per bond in capital appreciation, plus interest. Many chose not to cash out when the bonds were called (a convertible owner has the right to convert into common shares at any time rather than allow his bonds to be called). Those who did convert their bonds into shares at $32.50 a share saw those shares rise even more. It worked out to be a great long-term investment.

Could those investors have done better? Absolutely! Had they owned MCI common stock rather than the convertible bonds, their money would have grown by over 500 percent during the same period. The simple truth is that no one knows when or if a stock is going to go up. They did know that the convertible would pay 8.25 percent while they waited and that they would profit from any eventual appreciation. This is the tradeoff in convertible investing. Convertible holders recognize that if the stock is a stellar performer, in most cases they won't do as well as the common shareholder. But also keep in mind that the people who made the MCI convertible investment would have otherwise had that money parked in a money market fund. By investing in the MCI convertible instead, their return was well over twice as great. And had the price of the MCI stock fallen, the bonds would have provided some downside protection.

About the same time we began buying the MCI convertible, we also bought some convertible bonds issued by an airline. This stock turned out to be a laggard. The stock was trading around $8, where it remains today. The company's convertible bonds yielded 8 percent and still do. So investors who bought the bonds have been earning 8 percent on their money—even though the stock, which pays no dividend, has yet to move and money market rates have dropped to below 4 percent. We purchased these bonds at the same time that we bought the MCI bonds. MCI has been a big winner and the airline convertible bond hasn't done a thing. Even so, it's hard to consider the airline bond to be a loser. After all, investors are earning double money market rates on their money. Most are quite happy to be patient and wait for this investment to work out. Because no one knows which stock will move next, it is nice to be paid well during the wait. Convertible securities allow investors to do just that.

These two examples illustrate why convertibles are attractive to investors. Essentially, convertible securities offer a natural transition from savings certificates, Treasury notes and other fixed-income investments into assets that yield similar or better returns but offer something the others don't—upside potential. People who might otherwise be buying savings certificates or Treasuries can use convertibles to earn the same or higher rates while also giving their money a greater chance to grow rather than simply earn income.

Investors buy convertible securities either as alternatives for common stocks or as substitutes for straight bonds—or straight preferred stocks. When a convertible is purchased as a common stock substitute, its appreciation potential is of overriding importance. When a convertible is purchased as a fixed-income alternative, its yield is of primary concern. The bonus an investor receives by owning a convertible security is that he or she receives a combination of growth and income. The extent to which these growth and income properties exist for each convertible relates to the conversion features.

CHAPTER 2

Convertibles as Stock Substitutes

Good *convertible* investment ideas begin as good investment ideas. The only reason to own the convertible security rather than the common stock or straight bond is that the convertible represents the best value. A convertible is a tool like a wrench or a pair of pliers. Sometimes it makes sense to use a certain tool, and sometimes it makes sense to use something else. Sometimes a convertible is the best investment vehicle, and other times it isn't. Don't force its use. Use a convertible rather than the common stock or straight bond of the same company when it offers some advantage over the common or straight bond.

Remember the reasons that both the MCI and airline convertibles were chosen. Risk-averse investors wanted to earn the same rate of interest that they were earning in their money market funds but also wanted to give their money opportunity to grow. They were willing to invest in the convertible bonds because the interest they would earn from the bonds was similar to what they were already earning. They weren't interested in owning the common stock because the common stock paid no dividend. These investors regarded any appreciation as a bonus.

It is important to keep in mind that convertibles are alternative investments. An investor chooses to buy the convertible rather than the stock or bond of a company because there is some advantage to owning the convertible.

Chapter 8 discusses convertible investments that are bargains because they represent a special value. They may be mispriced, misunderstood, underappreciated or under-followed, but let's begin with the premise that the convertible represents the best way to invest in a company in which you want to invest.

So let's say you've made the decision to invest in the Caribbean Land Company (an imaginary outfit). You are curious to know whether a convertible security exists for the company.

HOW TO KNOW IF A COMPANY HAS A CONVERTIBLE

Once you identify a company in which you would like to invest, you can check several sources to discover whether that company has a convertible security. The fastest way is to ask your broker. You can also call the company's investor relations department. Here are several other sources:

Standard & Poor's. You can check the Standard & Poor's Corporation research sheets. They are available in most libraries and in the offices of most stock brokerage firms. If the company has a convertible, it will be noted under the capitalization section. Standard & Poor's also publishes a monthly bond guide that lists frequently traded convertible bonds. It is available at most stock brokerage firms or can be purchased directly from Standard & Poor's Corporation, 25 Broadway, New York, NY 10004, for $176 a year.

Investor's Business Daily. Every day, the financial newspaper *Investor's Business Daily* publishes a table of the 200 most actively traded convertibles from its universe of over 600 convertible bonds. It is listed under the heading "Super Convertible Bond Tables." The universe is updated three times a year to keep it current.

Moody's Bond Record. Moody's Bond Record is published monthly and can also be found in most libraries and stock brokerage offices. It is available from Moody's Investor Service, 99 Church Street, New York, NY 10007, for $175 a year. This is far more comprehensive than most services, following approximately 800 convertible bonds as well as thousands of other corporate and municipal securities. *Moody's Bond Survey* is a weekly publication about fixed-income securities, economic and market conditions, and new issues.

Most stock brokerage firms produce convertible research recommending specific issues. And a number of firms will indicate on the research pieces that they produce details regarding any convertible security issued by that company.

Value Line Convertible Service.   The most comprehensive lists are provided by *Value Line Convertible Service,* published 48 times a year by Value Line, Inc., 711 Third Avenue, New York, NY 10017. The subscription rate currently is $445 a year. The *Value Line Convertible Service* not only lists convertible securities but recommends specific issues and provides information about convertibles involved in mergers, tender offers, calls, changes in terms, exchange offers and expirations that affect convertible securities. The listing section is as complete as you will find anywhere. It includes information about the underlying common stock and facts about the convertible. *Value Line* evaluates each convertible, makes judgments as to market risk and projects price change based on change per point in the underlying common as well as per point in interest rates.

RHM Convertible Survey.   Another excellent source for convertible securities investors is the *RHM Convertible Survey,* published biweekly at 172 Forest Avenue, Glen Cove, NY 11542. The subscription rate currently is $350 a year. The RHM Convertible Survey also makes recommendations, and its tables are extraordinarily comprehensive. Both the Value Line and RHM publications are available at many libraries and brokerage firms.

BOND BASICS

Now comes the fun part. You found that there is a Caribbean Land Company convertible bond. It is described to you as a 6½ percent bond of 02 at 86. That kind of a description is probably enough to cause your eyes to glaze over and for you to decide to forget about the bond and buy the stock. But hold on! Let's figure out what it means.

Bonds are fixed-income instruments. The 6½ percent refers to the rate of interest the bond pays on its face value of $1,000 per year.

$$6½\% \times \$1,000 = \$65$$

This interest rate will not change during the life of the bond.

Bonds have limited lives. The term *02* refers to the end maturity in the year 2002. On Wall Street it is commonplace to omit the first two digits. A Caribbean Land Company bond with a January 1, 1998 maturity, for example, would probably be referred to as the Caribbean Lands of 98. Even the January 1 date would be omitted, meaning that this is the only Caribbean Land bond due in the year 1998. If two or more bonds were to mature in 1998, the month and date would be used.

In our example, the actual maturity of the Caribbean Land Company bond is January 1, 2002. That means that the bond will come due, and $1,000 per bond will be returned to the investor who owns that bond on January 1, 2002. The January 1 date is also an interest payment date. Most bonds pay interest twice a year; one-half of a year's interest is paid on the stated date, and the other half is paid six months from that date. This bond would pay one-half of $65 or $32.50 on January 1 and $32.50 on July 1 every year until maturity.

In the description of the bond that you received earlier the term *at 86* was used. This term refers to the price. Bonds are liquid investments. When you buy a bond you are the lender, but you can sell it to another investor. The bond price will change based on a number of factors. At this point, the bond's price is $860; "at 86" refers to a percent of face value. Bonds almost always mature at $1,000. At $1,000 the bond is trading at 100 percent of its face value. At 86 this bond is trading at 86 percent of its face value, $860. Bond prices are quoted in percentages. If you were to buy the bond at $860, the yield on your investment would be $65 ÷ $860 = 7.53 percent. That is referred to as the *current yield*. The stated yield of 6½ percent is called the *coupon yield*. When bonds were first sold to investors decades ago they had detachable coupons. Each coupon represented an interest payment. On the date that payment became due, a coupon was clipped from the bond and presented for payment. The term *coupon* survives from those times, and *coupon clippers* is a term still used by some to describe bond investors.

Comparison of Bonds at Discount, Premium and Par

At $860, the Caribbean Island Land bond is selling at a discount to its face or par value. If it were to trade above $1,000, it would be trading at a premium to its face value:

Current Market Value	Annual Interest	Current Yield
$ 86 (discount)	$65	7.53 percent
$110 (premium)	$65	5.90 percent
$100 (par)	$65	6.50 percent

Yield to Maturity

Discounts and premiums affect yield. If you buy a bond at either a discount or a premium to par you must take that into account to calculate the true return. For example, if you buy the bond at $860 and hold it until January 1, 2002, when it matures, you will receive $1,000 for each bond. As a result, your return will be higher than the stated rate of 6½ percent. You will also have earned $140 per bond ($1,000 – $860 = $140).

If you paid a premium for the bond, your true return would be less than 6½ percent. In both instances the yield will be affected by the number of years to maturity. In the case of the bond purchased at $860, if there were ten years to maturity your true return would be $65 a year in stated interest plus $14 a year in average appreciation. The $14 is arrived at by dividing the $140 gain by the ten years it will take to realize the gain.

Had you paid $110 for the same bond, over a ten year period, you would lose $100, or $10 a year. Your true return would be $55 a year ($65 – $10 = $55). The yield calculation that takes these kinds of gains and losses into effect is called *yield to maturity*.

AND NOW, CONVERTIBLE BONDS

All of these terms apply to convertible bonds as well as to straight bonds. Convertible bonds have maturities, stated interest rates and interest payment dates. They can trade at discounts and premiums to their par value. Convertible bonds also have a conversion feature. The conversion feature is the bond owner's right to exchange or convert the bond into another asset. Convertible bonds can be converted into any number of different types of assets, but let's begin with the basics.

The Caribbean Land Company 6½ percent bond due January 1, 2002, can be converted into 50 common shares of the Caribbean Land Company. The *conversion ratio* is the number of shares into which the bond can be converted. In this instance the conversion ratio is 50 shares. The *conversion price* is the price per share at which the bond can be converted. In this example, the conversion price is $20.

The *conversion value* is the number of shares into which the convertible security can be exchanged, multiplied by the current price of those shares. When the shares are trading at $20, the conversion value of the Caribbean Land Company bond is equal to $1,000 ($20 × 50 shares = $1,000). Because the conversion value changes as the current price of the shares into which the convertible bond can be exchanged changes, the convertible takes on a different characteristic from a straight or nonconvertible bond. (See Figure 2.1.)

Let's review what we know about the Caribbean Land Company 6½s of 02:

- We know it is a bond that pays $65 per year in interest.
- We know it matures in 2002 at $1,000 per bond.
- We know that it is convertible into 50 shares of Caribbean Land Company common stock at any time we choose.

Because this bond can be converted into a specific number of common stock shares, the bond takes on some of the characteristics of the stock into which it can be converted. For example, what do you suppose would happen to the bond's value if the shares of the Caribbean Land company were to rise to $25 a share? If you answered that the value of the bond would also rise, you understand the concept. If

FIGURE 2.1   Relationship of Stock Price to Conversion Value

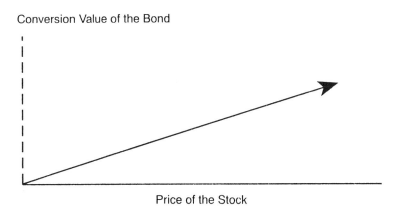

Conversion Value of the Bond

Price of the Stock

As the price of the common stock rises, so will the conversion value of the bond.

the price of the stock is $25 and the convertible bond can be converted to 50 shares, the value of the bond would be equal to 50 shares × $25, or $1,250. That price is referred to as *conversion parity* or simply *parity*. A convertible bond will never trade (be valued at) below its conversion parity.

Considering further how conversion parity works, remember that as the Caribbean Land Company's common share value rises, so too will the price of the Caribbean Land Company's convertible bond:

Share Price		*Conversion Ratio*		*Conversion Parity*
$20	×	50	=	$1,000
$25	×	50	=	$1,250
$30	×	50	=	$1,500
$40	×	50	=	$2,000

As the price of the common stock declines, so too would the conversion parity of the convertible bond:

Share price		Conversion Ratio		Conversion Parity
$20	×	50	=	$1,000
$15	×	50	=	$ 750
$10	×	50	=	$ 500
$ 5	×	50	=	$ 250

In real life, convertibles almost never trade at parity. The real price of the Caribbean Land Company convertible bonds will be higher than the parity price. That is, they will trade at a premium to their conversion parity. The reasons for that are that the bond's fixed interest rate, its fixed maturity value and its senior status in the company's capital structure hierarchy give additional value to the convertible security.

Remember that the bond pays $65 a year in interest. Convertible bonds almost always pay a higher return than the same amount of money invested in the company's stock. Let's assume that the Caribbean Land Company's common stock pays an annual dividend of 50 cents a share. It is an arbitrary number, but it illustrates a point that is almost always true. *Convertibles pay more than the common stock into which they can be converted.*

Since the Caribbean Land Company bond can be converted into 50 shares and each share pays a 50-cent dividend, the annual amount of income an investor would receive by holding 50 shares would be $25 a year. The bond pays $65 a year. Only if the value of the convertible bond were to rise above $1,625 would 50 shares of the stock pay more than the bond. This is why:

$$\$1,625 \times 2\tfrac{1}{2}\% = \$65$$

Remember also that dividend payment can be adjusted by a corporation both up and down, while the interest paid by a bond is fixed.

That is an interesting concept to understand because in considering when it makes sense to convert a bond into stock, the possibility of earning a higher return is one of the reasons. However, tuck it in the back of your mind for now. The point at issue is that *convertible bonds almost always trade above parity,* and the higher income is one reason.

The second reason is that convertibles have a fixed maturity date. That becomes important if the conversion value of the bond is below $1,000. Assume the Caribbean Land Company common stock was trading at $15 a share. The conversion value of the bond would be $750 ($15 × 50 shares = $750). Simply because the bond will mature at $1,000, the price of the bond will almost always be above $750 (unless the Caribbean Land Company is in such financial difficulty that its ability to redeem the bond is in doubt). There is an exception to this rule that will be explained in greater detail in the section that deals with convertibles as bond substitutes. Quite simply, it has to do with yield to maturity. If the yield to maturity of similar bonds is higher than the yield to maturity of the Caribbean Land Company bond priced at $750 (its conversion value) the bond can trade at its conversion value. It is an unlikely scenario because both the conversion feature, which gives some value to the possibility that the share price could go up, and the yield combine to cause the price of the convertible to almost always trade above its conversion value. This is a characteristic of a convertible security that makes it unique.

The third reason that the Caribbean Land Company's convertible will almost always trade above its conversion value is its position in the hierarchy on the company's balance sheet. The hierarchy of a corporation's capital structure can be seen in this ranking of the most senior to the most junior corporate obligees:

1. Bondholders
2. Convertible bondholders
3. Preferred shareholders
4. Preference shareholders
5. Convertible preferred shareholders
6. Common shareholders

The significance of the capital hierarchy doesn't mean much to anyone unless the company is in financial trouble. If there is a financial problem, the order of each claim on the company's assets becomes significant. Bondholders are creditors of the company. The common shareholders are owners. Creditors are entitled to be paid what they are owed before the owners receive anything.

If the company prospers, the creditors or debt holders are entitled only to what is owed them, nothing more. Common stock shareholders benefit from profits. High profits usually mean higher common share prices and can mean higher common share dividends.

CONVERSION PREMIUM

Though it is a fact that convertible bonds almost always trade at a premium to their conversion value, this is probably a good place for a definition. The difference between the market price of a convertible bond and its conversion value is called a *conversion premium.* Assume that the market price of the Caribbean Land Company common stock is $25 a share. The conversion value is $1,250 (50 shares × $25 = $1,250). Assume that the market price of the Caribbean Land 6½s of 02 is $1,300. We know that $1,250 is the conversion value. In a situation such as this one the conversion premium is a critical tool used in evaluating the desirability of a convertible security. The size of the conversion premium is always measured as a percentage. In this case the bond is trading at $1,300. To find the conversion premium, subtract the conversion value ($1,250) from $1,300. The difference is $50. Divide the difference by the conversion value ($50 ÷ $1,250 = 4%). The conversion premium in this case is 4 percent. Convertible investors generally consider any conversion premium of 25 percent or less as desirable. The smaller the conversion premium, the more the convertible will trade like the common stock into which it can be converted. The effect of a small conversion premium is that the price of the convertible will move up roughly in line with the price of the common stock. If the conversion premium is large, a movement in the common share price will have little effect on the price of the convertible. That concept is illustrated in Figure 2.2.

Having determined the amount of the conversion premium, an investor will want to know how long he or she will need to own the convertible to justify paying a premium over its conversion parity. That is calculated by determining the *breakeven period.*

FIGURE 2.2   Example of Large and Small Conversion Premiums

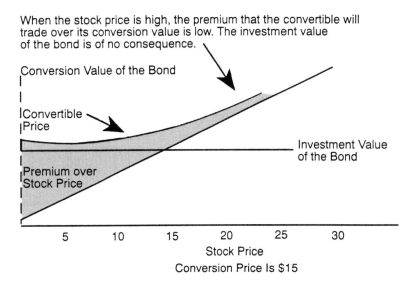

When the stock price is high, the premium that the convertible will trade over its conversion value is low. The investment value of the bond is of no consequence.

Conversion Value of the Bond

Convertible Price

Investment Value of the Bond

Premium over Stock Price

5   10   15   20   25   30

Stock Price

Conversion Price Is $15

When the stock price is low the premium that the convertible will trade over its conversion value is high. The convertible's price is a function of the bond's investment value. Very little value is given to the conversion feature.

The breakeven period represents the time it will take the income advantage of the convertible bond over the stock to offset the premium paid to acquire the convertible bond rather than the common stock. In other words, the breakeven period represents the number of years it would take for the extra yield offered by the convertible to offset the conversion premium.

Back to our example. The Caribbean Land Company convertible pays a 6½ percent rate of interest on its face value, or $65 a year, while the common pays a 25 cents per share dividend. Since each bond may be converted into 50 shares, an investor forgoes $12.50 worth of dividends (50 shares × .25 dividend per share) by owning the bond rather than the common stock. Thus, his or her *income advantage* in owning the bond over the stock is equal to $52.50 ($65 bond interest − $12.50 stock dividend). The breakeven period is computed by dividing the conversion premium by the income advantage offered by the bond. In this case, $50.00 ÷ $52.50 = .75 years.

In this example, after nine months an investor will have recovered the premium paid to buy the convertible. From that time on, the additional income received by owning the convertible bond rather than the common is a true benefit. Convertibles with small conversion premiums and short breakeven periods can be regarded as investments you might have otherwise made in the same company's stock. Those with large conversion premiums and long breakeven periods generally pay higher returns and are considered substitutes for the company's straight bonds.

CONVERTIBLE PREFERRED SHARES

To this point, we have considered bonds that can be converted into common stock shares. Another frequently issued convertible security is called a *convertible preferred* or sometimes *convertible preference* stock. Unlike bonds, these stocks have no fixed maturity and need never be repaid by the issuer. Like bonds, they pay a fixed interest rate , usually quarterly. Because they are stocks rather than bonds, that income is called a dividend rather than interest. Preferred and preference shares are most often offered in $100, $50, $25 or $10 denominations. Preferred stock ranks below bonds and ahead of preference shares, which, in turn, rank ahead of common stock in a corporation's capital structure.

Assume that the Caribbean Land Company issued a convertible preferred stock. Assume also that it was priced at $50 a share. That price is referred to as *par*, just as $1,000 is called a bond's *par price*. If someone quoted a bond's price to you "at par" you would understand that meant the bond was trading at $1,000. The par price of a preferred share might be $100, $50, $25 or even $10, depending on the price at which it was originally issued (sold to investors). Because preferred stock issues never mature, the par price is not a big deal except as it relates to how the company can *call* (take the stock) from an investor (more about this later).

In this example, the Caribbean Land Company convertible preferred pays a $3-a-share dividend. Unlike a bond that is described by using the rate of interest it pays and maturity date (i.e., Caribbean Land 6½s of 02), a preferred issue is described by using the dollar amount of the dividend it pays. In this case it is called the Caribbean Land Company's $3 convertible preferred. It may also be referred to with a letter of the alphabet. The first preferred issued by the company is the Caribbean Land Company's $3 A convertible preferred. The second issue, if there were one, would be the series B preferred. The third would be the series C preferred and so on. In the hierarchy of the corporation's capital structure the series A preferred would be senior to series B and so on.

Another term that investors are confronted with when dealing with preferred stocks is *cumulative*. A *cumulative preferred* is one that accumulates dividends owed but not paid. If, because of financial difficulty, the Caribbean Land Company were unable to make dividend payments on its cumulative preferred issue, these owed but not paid dividends would nonetheless remain obligations of the corporation. By law, a company with any of these obligations outstanding would not be allowed to pay any dividend to the common shareholders until the unpaid cumulative preferred dividends had been paid. When they are paid, they are paid to whomever owns the cumulative preferred stock at the time. (Chapter 8 describes how some of these preferreds have been terrific investments because of this characteristic and how to look for those that exist now.)

The stock listing for a Series A cumulative convertible preferred would look like this:

Caribbean Land Company $3.00 Cm Cv A Pfd

The conversion ratio is also expressed somewhat differently for a convertible preferred stock than for a convertible bond. Remember, with the Caribbean Land Company's 6½s of 02, the conversion ratio is 50. Each bond is convertible into 50 shares of Caribbean Land Company common stock. With the Caribbean Land Company cumulative convertible series A preferred stock, the conversion ratio is (in this example) 2.5. That means each convertible preferred share can be exchanged for 2.5 common shares. The conversion price is $20 (2.5 × conversion price = $50).

Let's consider how the terms *conversion premium* and *breakeven* apply to convertible preferred shares. It will be easy to grasp, as the concept is the same. If the Caribbean Land Company convertible series A preferred is trading at $60, the conversion premium is $10 ($60 − $50 = $10), or 20 percent ($10 ÷ $50 = 20%).

We know that at any time, as owners of this Caribbean Land Company preferred stock, we have the right to convert it into 2.5 shares of Caribbean Land Company common. In this example, the common stock is trading at $20, so the conversion value is 2.5 × $20 = $50. Since the preferred is trading at $60, the difference between the conversion value and the current price of the preferred is $10 ($60 current value − $50 conversion value = $10).

To make sure you understand this concept, follow these price changes as they apply to changes in the conversion premium.

Example 1
- Assume the common price remains at $20, but the preferred price rises to $65.
- Conversion value equals $20 current price × 2.5 conversion ratio = $50.
- Conversion premium equals $65 market price of the preferred − $50 conversion price = $15.
- Expressed as a percentage, $15 conversion premium ÷ $50 conversion price = 30%.

Example 2
- Assume the common price rises to $25, and the preferred price remains at $65.
- Conversion value equals $25 current price × 2.5 conversion ratio = $62.50.
- Conversion premium equals $65 market price of the preferred − $62.50 conversion value = $2.50.
- Expressed as a percentage, $2.50 conversion premium ÷ $62.50 conversion price = 4%.

Example 3
- Assume the common price is at $18, and the preferred price is at $56.
- Conversion value equals $18 current price × 2.5 conversion ratio = $45.
- Conversion premium equals $56 market price of the preferred – $45 conversion ratio = $11.
- Expressed as a percentage, $11 conversion premium ÷ $45 conversion value = 24.4%.

It is important to remember that *the conversion ratio is the constant.* The number of common shares into which the convertible preferred can be exchanged never changes even though the prices of the preferred shares and the common shares will change. The other constant is the dividend. The amount of the preferred dividend doesn't change even though the price of the preferred share will. In this example the dividend is $3 a share. That amount is payable whether the share price is $15, $20 or $25.

The breakeven period is determined for a convertible preferred share just as it is with a convertible bond. To illustrate how it works, let's take our last example where the Caribbean Land Company common share price is at $18, the conversion premium is $11, the preferred stock dividend is $3 and the common stock dividend is 25 cents per year.

Because each of the convertible preferred shares can be exchanged into 2.5 shares of common, the investor forgoes 62.5 cents of dividends (2.5 × $.25 = $.625) by investing in the preferred rather than owning the common shares. The income advantage in owning the preferred is $2.375 ($3 preferred dividend – $.625 common stock dividend). The breakeven period is computed by dividing the conversion premium by the income advantage offered by the preferred. In this case, $11.00 ÷ 2.37 = 4.64 years.

In this example, after 4.64 years, an investor will have recovered the premium paid to buy the convertible preferred rather than the common. From that time on, the additional income received by owning the convertible preferred is a true benefit.

BONDS OR PREFERREDS—WHICH IS BETTER?

A fair question might be: Given the choice, should an investor choose to own a convertible bond or a convertible preferred of the same company? The answer is that there is rarely the choice. It is quite unusual to find a company that offers both. The main point is there may be one or the other. Don't give up your search for an issuer's convertible security by checking for only a convertible bond or only a convertible preferred. They are often listed in separate sections of financial newspapers.

If there are choices of convertible issues, an investor's goal is to determine which is the better value. As you read on you will learn how. However, a rule to begin with is *the smaller the conversion premium the more the convertible will take on the characteristics of the underlying common stock.* Investors who choose to own a convertible rather than the common look for small, ideally microscopic premiums. The smaller the conversion premium, the more its price will move with the common shares into which it can be converted.

This is why. Assume our Caribbean Land Company 6½s of 02 are trading at 85 ($850). Remember that they are convertible into 50 shares of the underlying common. Assume further that the common is trading at $16 a share. The conversion value is $800:

$16 Market price of the common × 50 Shares conversion
ratio = $800 Conversion value

The conversion premium is $50, or 6.25 percent:

$850 Market price of the convertible bonds – $800
Conversion value = $50 Conversion premium

$$\$50 \div \$800 = 6.25\%$$

Because the conversion premium is so small (6.25%), if the stock price moved up to $17 a share the conversion value would be $17 × 50 = $850. Just to maintain the same 6.25 premium—*convertibles always trade at a premium to their conversion value*—the convertible bond would trade at:

$903 Market price of the convertible bond – $850
Conversion value = $53 Conversion premium

$$\$53 \div \$850 = 6.25\%$$

On the other hand, assume the Caribbean Land Company 6½s of 02 are trading at 85 ($850) and the common is at $6. The conversion value is $300:

$6 Market price of the common × 50 Shares conversion ratio = $300 Conversion value

The conversion premium is $550 or 183%:

$850 Market price of the convertible bond – $300
Conversion value = $550 Conversion premium

$$\$550 \div \$300 = 183\%$$

If the common stock price moved up from $6 to $7 the conversion value would be $350:

$7 Market price of the common × 50 Shares conversion ratio = $350 Conversion value

Assuming the price of the bond remained at $850, the conversion premium is 143%:

$850 Market price of the convertible bond – $350
Conversion value = $500 Conversion premium

$$\$500 \div \$350 = 143\%$$

While 143 percent is a smaller premium than 183 percent, it is still so big that the bond's price is unlikely to move up much at all as the price of the common rises. The value of being able to convert this bond for common stock at a conversion premium of 143 percent isn't much more attractive than 183 percent. Frankly, its conversion value isn't worth much. This bond is attractive for another reason: its income. At $850 with a 6½ percent coupon, this bond's current yield is 7.6 percent. Let us consider next why convertibles are attractive as income investments.

CHAPTER 3

Convertibles as Bond or Preferred Stock Substitutes

These are the three most important reasons convertible securities are attractive common stock substitutes:

1. *A convertible will appreciate in value as the underlying common stock appreciates.*
2. *A convertible almost always pays a higher return than the underlying common stock.*

   This is an important convertible characteristic because no one knows when a common stock will appreciate. Being paid well while waiting for that to happen increases the odds of turning in a respectable year-after-year investment performance.
3. *A convertible offers a safety net to protect investors, should the underlying common stock suffer a sharp price decline.*

   This downside protection is provided by the income from the convertible. Should the price of the common stock fall, the price of the convertible security shouldn't fall as much as the common and can be expected to decline in value only to the point where it yields a return comparable to a nonconvertible security of similar maturity and quality.

In the case of the Caribbean Land Company, 6½s of 02 priced at $850 with the common stock price at $7, the conversion premium is a whopping 143 percent. The current yield, however, is 7.6 percent.

This bond is priced as it is because similar bonds also yield around 7.6 percent. That is, bonds issued for similar companies of similar quality are paying a similar return. At this time, 7.6 percent is the prevailing rate of interest paid by companies like the Caribbean Land Company to borrow money.

The Caribbean Land Company bond has another feature that adds to its appeal: its ability to be converted into Caribbean Land Company common stock. Even though, as pointed out, that conversion feature isn't as attractive as it would be if the common stock price were higher, it still exists and has some value. This bond would be more attractive than the straight or nonconvertible bond if it paid approximately the same interest rate because the ability to convert might, if the common stock goes up in price, become a valuable bonus.

The fact that the bond is trading at $850, where it yields approximately what other bonds of similar characteristics yield, is another attraction of convertible securities. It is referred to as a *double floor.* The first level of price support, or *floor*, below which the bond should not trade, is the conversion value. Because an investor can exchange the bond for a fixed number of shares of the underlying common and sell those shares at their market price, the convertible bond will not trade below its conversion parity.

The second floor, or level of price support, is provided by the yield. As mentioned a number of times, the Caribbean Land Company bond will always trade where other bonds of similar characteristics will trade.

This is why. Assume that you have $10,000 to invest. You want to earn income with your money and you want to know that after a certain period of time you will get your money back. You could buy a savings certificate, put money in a money market fund or buy a U.S. Treasury security or corporate bond.

You decide to buy a $10,000 U.S. Treasury note. The rate of interest paid by Treasuries and all fixed-income investments changes over time based on a number of economic reasons. (See Figure 3.1.) In this instance, the rate of interest paid by the ten-year Treasury bond that you bought is 7½ percent. Like clockwork, every

FIGURE 3.1   Fixed-Rate Straight Bond

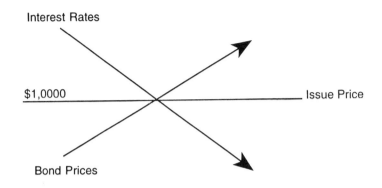

The price of a fixed-rate bond and changing interest rates always go in opposite directions.

six months you receive an interest check for half a year's interest, and as the years pass the maturity date grows closer.

Assume it is four years later and for some reason you need to sell your Treasury bond. Interest rates have risen some during those four years. The bond you need to sell now is a six-year Treasury bond yielding 7½ percent. Four of the ten years toward the maturity date have passed. Therefore, the Treasury bond you own is not a ten-year bond anymore but a six-year bond. Because interest rates have gone up, new six-year Treasury bonds yield 8 percent. Do you think that your bond will sell for

- $10,000?
- less than $10,000?
- more than $10,000?

Keep in mind that an investor can buy a new six-year U.S. Treasury bond at 8 percent and that your bond, with six years to maturity, has a 7½ percent coupon.

The price that your bond will command in the market will be less than $10,000. It will sell at a discount to its face value. The amount of the discount will equal enough to cause your bond to yield 8 percent to the buyer. If 8 percent is the prevailing interest rate paid by six-year U.S. Treasury bonds, all six-year U.S. Treasury bonds will trade at a price that causes them to yield 8 percent.

WHAT CAUSES BOND PRICES TO FLUCTUATE?

Bond prices are affected by changes in the prevailing interest rates and also by the financial stability of the issuer. In the U.S. Treasury example, the price changes result only from interest rate changes. There is no concern in the market price about the quality of the U.S. Treasury.

With the Caribbean Land Company bonds and all corporate bonds there will be market price questions about the company's financial health. To help investors evaluate a company's financial health, there are bond rating services. The three *major rating services* are:

1. Moody's Investor Service
    99 Church Street
    New York, NY 10007
2. Standard & Poor's Corporation (S&P)
    26 Broadway
    New York, NY 10004
3. Fitch Investors Service
    5 Hanover Square
    New York, NY 10004

Each rating service examines the financial stability of the issuer, its history of repayment and the collateral, if any, of the bond. The service then assigns a rating to each bond and publishes the rating. This rating is a judgment of the issuer's credit quality.

A bond's rating tells you how safe it is. The rating is a determination of the issuer's financial strength and its ability to repay principal and to make its interest payments. It is an estimation of the credit risk of the issuer. It offers no judgment on the prospective return of such an investment. Figure 3.2 illustrates the bond rating system of the three agencies.

Bonds rated AAA (Aaa), AA, A, or BBB (Baa) are called *investment grade* (or bank quality). There is very little risk of default with these bonds.

Bonds rated below investment grade are often referred to as junk bonds because of the risk inherent in investing in low-quality bonds.

THE MEANING OF RATING SYMBOLS

- AAA (Aaa)—highest quality—The issuer has exceptional ability to repay.
- AA (Aa)—high quality—The issuer has very strong ability to repay.
- A—good quality—The issuer has strong ability to repay.

FIGURE 3.2 Bond Ratings

Description	Moody's	S&P	Fitch
Highest Quality	Aaa	AAA	AAA
	As	AA	AA
	A	A	A
Medium Quality	Baa	BBB	BBB
	Ba	BB	BB
	B	B	B
Poor Quality	Caa	CCC	CCC
	Ca	CC	CC
	C	C	C
Lowest Quality		D	DDD
			DD
			D

- BBB (Baa)—satisfactory quality—The issuer has adequate ability to repay.
- BB (Ba)—below investment grade, considered as speculative—The issuer's ability to repay is not strong.
- B—highly speculative—The issuer's ability to repay is questionable.
- CCC (Caa)—The bond is vulnerable to default.
- CC (Ca)—The bond is minimally protected; default seems probable.
- C—The bond is in default or default is imminent.
- DDD, DD, and D—In default; to be purchased for liquidation value only.

The actual definitions used by each rating service may vary slightly, but the purpose is clear. A change from one rating level to another indicates a slightly higher or lower opinion concerning the safety of that bond as an investment.

Each service has additional rating codes or symbols to further explain its ratings. For example, Standard & Poor's and Fitch use these signals:

- (+) or (–)—These symbols appear after the rating to indicate finer distinctions of positive or negative opinion.
- NR—A rating was not requested or was not completed in time for publication.
- SUSPENDED—The rating is suspended because the information is inadequate.
- WITHDRAWN—The rating is withdrawn because the issuer did not supply timely information.
- CONDITIONAL—The rating is conditional, based on assumptions about timely completion of a project being financed by the bond issue.
- ALERT—The issue is under review, and a change in the rating is possible. An ALERT may be UP (positive implication); DOWN (negative implication); or EVOLVING (the direction of the change in rating is not certain).

The statement was made that the Caribbean Land Company bonds would trade at approximately the same price as other bonds with similar characteristics. If we say that a Caribbean Land Company bond is single A-rated we can assume that it will trade at approximately the same price as other A-rated bonds with a 6½ percent coupon and a 2002 maturity. If it traded precisely where other non-convertible bonds of the same characteristics trade, it would trade at its *investment value.* Because it is a convertible bond, there will be some worth given to its conversion feature, so you can expect it to trade at a premium to its pure investment value. The price represented by a bond's investment value is the second floor of the double floor for a convertible security. The first is that the convertible will not trade below its conversion value. The second is that a convertible will not trade below its investment value.

Figure 3.3 shows the double floor. As the price of the common stock rises, so will the conversion value of the bond. The investment value of the bond is dependent on changing interest rates. A convertible will never sell below its investment value or its conversion value, whichever is lower.

FIGURE 3.3   The Double Floor

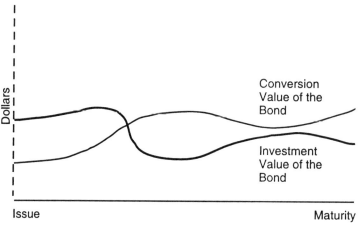

A convertible will never trade below either its investment value or its conversion value, whichever is higher.

CHAPTER 4

What Can Go Wrong and How To Keep Problems from Happening to You

Once you own a convertible security, you must pay particular attention to its *call provisions* because call provisions affect how the convertible can be taken from you. All convertibles can be called or redeemed, that is, repurchased by the issuer at a specific price. The call price is established at the time the convertible is issued. Sometimes the call price adjusts downward over a number of years. For example, the convertible bond may be callable at 102 ($1,020) for the first five years after it is issued and then at 100 ($1,000) for the balance of its life.

Sometimes an investor's protection from a call is absolute and sometimes it is provisional. *Absolute call protection,* also referred to as hard call protection, means the issue cannot be called for any reason until the call date.

Convertibles with *provisional call protection,* or soft call protection, can be called if certain circumstances occur. An example of a convertible bond with a soft call is the Caribbean Land Company 5⅜ percent convertible bond due to mature September 1, 2003. This bond cannot be called until September 1, 1996, unless Caribbean Land Company common stock reaches $40 a share and remains at that price or higher for 20 out of 30 consecutive stock trading days. The likelihood of this bond's being called is a direct function of how well the common stock performs. That is why it is called a provisional, or soft, call as opposed to a hard call.

Call protection is important because convertible investors buy converts rather than the underlying common for their higher yield. If the underlying common stock climbed sharply shortly after an investor bought the convertible, and the company was able to call the bond immediately, an investor could lose the yield advantage of owning the convert. Good call protection allows an investor to hold onto the bond and enjoy the high return while also benefitting from the appreciation of the common.

An issue with good call protection will always trade with a higher conversion premium and thereby be a better investment than one with poor call protection. This is why. Assume that we own the Caribbean Land Company 6⅜ percent converts, which are convertible into 40 shares of common at $21.22 per share. The common is currently trading at $29.37, and the convertible bond is trading at $1,287.50. The bond is trading at nearly a 10 percent conversion premium because it has hard call protection until November 2, 1996. If it didn't, the bond would trade with little or no premium to its conversion parity because the stock is trading well above the bond's conversion price. That is logical because if the convertible were called, an investor would lose the premium that was paid to buy it.

If you own a convertible that can be called at any time, you must pay attention to how much over the conversion value the convertible is trading. If the issue is called, you stand to lose the difference between the market price of the issue and its conversion value, or parity.

Remember that the right to convert into common shares belongs to the convertible owner. So if, in this instance, the bond were called, the convertible owner would have the right to convert the bond into the common shares. As a result, he or she could continue to be an investor in the company. That is a convertible owner's right. What he or she would have lost is the amount of money above the conversion price that the bond was trading. This is how that works. Prior to the call, the bond was trading at $1,287.50. Its conversion value is 40 shares × $29.37, or $1,174.80. The moment the bond is called, it is worth either the call price or the conversion value, whichever is greater. No one will pay more, so the market value will immediately drop from $1,287.50 to $1,174.80.

WHAT HAPPENS IF YOUR CONVERTIBLE IS CALLED

In real life, this is what happens when a convertible is called. In early 1990, a company called Conner Peripherals called its 9 percent convertibles due to mature in the year 2014. Like all other calls, it was a surprise. At the time of the call, the Conner converts were trading at $1,980 each. Call notices appeared in major financial newspapers such as *The Wall Street Journal* and *Investor's Business Daily*. They were also mailed by the company to each convert bond holder, or if the converts were held in a brokerage account, a notice was sent to each investor by the investor's broker.

Notices begin by referring to the provisions of the bond indenture that allows the company to call or redeem its bond. The notice lists the price at which the bonds will be redeemed and the redemption date. In the case of the Conner convertibles, the redemption price was $1,081 per $1,000 principal amount. The date was May 3, 1990. If an investor simply allowed his bonds to be redeemed, he would be paid interest from the last interest payment date plus $1,081 for each bond. Sometimes an investor is not paid the accrued interest owed until the redemption date. For example, if a bond pays interest on May 1 and November 1 and the bond is called for redemption on April 20, the bondholder will lose the nearly six months' interest owed to that date. That is because the investor will not own the bond on May 1, the interest payment date.

If an investor continues to hold his bonds beyond the redemption date, interest will cease to accrue and the bonds will no longer carry the right to be converted into the common. So doing nothing does no good at all. The investment stops earning interest and ceases to have any relation to the price movement of the underlying common shares. The bondholder's only right after that date is to tender the bonds to the company at the redemption price.

Failing to take action can be a big mistake. More than a few convertible holders have missed redemption dates and lost money as a result. The company, after all, is under no obligation to pay more than the redemption price. How expensive that can be is illustrated by using the Conner bonds as an example.

The Conner Peripheral convertible bond could be converted at the conversion price of $9.85 a share into 101.523 shares of common stock. Since the common at the time was trading at $18.75, the convertible bond had an investment value of $1,903.56 (101.523 × $18.75 = $1,903.56). Obviously, allowing the bond to be redeemed at $1,081 was not a good choice. Conner convert holders would have been better off either converting or selling the bond, which, as a result of the call, was trading at conversion parity ($1,903.56 per bond). If the bond were to be redeemed, the investor would forgo $822.56 per bond ($1,903.56 − $1,081 = $822.56).

Let's say an investor missed the redemption notice and didn't sell or convert the bonds. His only option would be to redeem the bonds with the company at $1,081 each. Plenty of owners of millions of dollars' worth of bonds have done just that. Companies have refused, as they have had every right to do, to allow late conversions into the common, and investors have suffered for being inattentive.

This is a strong argument for leaving your convertibles on deposit in your brokerage account at a reputable brokerage firm rather than storing them in a safe deposit box. A brokerage firm will help you monitor your convertible securities and notify you about redemptions and calls. A knowledgeable broker will be available as well to discuss your options—to sell or convert—when you are faced with either a redemption or a call.

WHAT TO DO IN THE EVENT OF A CALL

Allowing the bond to be called doesn't make sense, and selling the bond quickly to capture the premium over the call price isn't possible. That leaves two options: either sell the bond or convert the bond into the underlying common stock. By doing the latter, each of the bonds is convertible into 40 shares of the common stock. Because the stock is selling at $29.37 a share, the value of the stock upon conversion is $1,174.80 ($29.37 a share × 40 shares per bond).

If you decide to sell the bond, sell it before you convert into the common stock because the brokerage fee to sell a bond is almost always lower than the brokerage fee to sell the stock. And the best time to do it is immediately. Most of the convertible holders are institutional owners or mutual funds. Most do not want to hold the common stock, so you can expect to see the price of the common decline as they sell out. Because the market for the common is more liquid than the market for the convertibles, many of the institutions will sell the underlying stock immediately and not wait for the conversion to occur. That puts pressure on the price of the stock. It is hard for an institution to dump a multimillion-dollar convertible position in the market for an issue that has already been called. Who wants it? An individual with 10 or 20 thousand dollars to sell doesn't face the same position.

The price you will get from an immediate sale will probably be higher than it would have been if you had waited to sell the stock until after the conversion. And because you have a modest position in the convertible compared to the institutional holders, the convertible marketplace, whether bond or preferred, should be plenty liquid for you.

WHEN IS THE ISSUER LIKELY TO CALL THE CONVERTIBLE?

A general rule is that the issuer is more likely to call a convertible when its market price is 15 to 20 percent above its call price. However, the right to call belongs solely to the issuer, and plenty of convertibles have been called when trading well below a 15 to 20 percent premium to the call price.

A good rule to apply is: How painful would it be to you if the issue were called? This has to do with how much you would stand to lose if the convertible were taken from you. This must be continually assessed. If you own a convertible that is callable, you should frequently compute the spread between the market price and the conversion value. Ask yourself how uncomfortable you would be to lose that spread, because you will lose it if the issue is called.

Take into account the yield advantage of owning the convertible versus the underlying common into which it could be converted. If the yield advantage of owning the convertible is small, and the spread between the market price and conversion value is large, you should sell the convertible and buy shares of the common rather than risk losing the spread to a call.

This is how that could work to an investor's advantage. Assume that you own the Caribbean Land Company 6½s of 02 trading at 180. Assume that the bonds are convertible into 40 shares of the common and that the common is trading at \$37.50. The conversion value is \$37.50 × 40 = \$1,500. The bonds are trading at a 20 percent premium to their conversion value: \$1,800 − \$1,500 ÷ 1,500 = 20 percent.

The bond pays \$65 a year. The shares pay a \$.50 per share annual dividend. If the bond were called, the investor would lose \$300 per bond (\$1,800 − \$1,500 = \$300). If the investor sold the bond at \$1,800 and used the proceeds to buy shares at \$37.50 each, he would own 48 shares: \$1,800 ÷ 37.50 = 48 shares. If the bond were called, the investor would own 40 shares. Forty-eight shares produces an annual dividend of \$24, versus the \$65 from the bond. While there is a \$41 (\$65 − \$24 = \$41) annual income advantage in owning the bond, if the bond were called, the lost premium would be worth 7.31 years of income advantage (\$300 ÷ \$41.00 = 7.31). An investor stands to lose too much from a call in this instance and should sell the convertible to prevent that from happening.

The point is that if you own a convertible that is callable you must make judgments continually about the advisability of continuing to hold that security.

THE RISK OF A BUYOUT

The value of a convertible security can be adversely affected by a merger or buyout of the issuing company. To illustrate this point, assume that we are considering buying the Caribbean Land Company bond. The price of the bond is \$450. Its face interest rate is 6 percent. The price of the Caribbean Land Company common stock is $4.50 a share. The bond is convertible at $30 into 33.33 shares. Its conversion value is $150 ($4.50 × 33.33 = $150). The conversion premium is 200 percent. The price of the bond, $450, minus the conversion value of the bond, $150, equals $300, which, divided by $150, equals 200 percent.

A major risk of owning a convertible bond trading well below its conversion price is that the company might be acquired by another firm at a price below the conversion price. What if, for example, someone offered $9 a share for the Caribbean Land Company shares? The common shareholders probably would be delighted because their $4.50-a-share stock would be worth $9 a share. However, the convertible bond holders would be losers. Because the bond can be converted into 33.33 shares of the common, a $9-a-share offer would make each bond worth only $300 ($9 × 33.33 shares = $300). A buyout at double the common share price in this instance would mean a loss of $150 per bond for the convertible investor ($450 – $300 = $150), if the convertible bond owner were to convert.

The convertible bond owner is not required to convert his or her bond into common stock. He or she could simply continue to hold the bond. And because it pays $60 a year interest, the yield would probably keep the bond from trading as low as its conversion parity ($300). However, the takeover would eliminate the bond's conversion value. Because the buyout was at $9 a share, the stock will never trade at $30. After the takeover, the company will not exist as a separate entity. So it will trade from that time on like every other nonconvertible bond of similar yield and quality.

The classic illustration of the impact of a takeover on the value of a convertible security involves the convertible bonds of Wherehouse Entertainment, Inc. Wherehouse issued a 6¼ percent convertible due 2006, at a time when Wherehouse common stock was trading at $22 a share. Each of these bonds could be converted for a fraction over 36 shares. The conversion price was $27.60 a share. After the convertible was issued, the stock began to fall in price, never again to trade at $27 or any price remotely close. Over time, the stock sank from $22 to $13. With the common trading at $13 and the bond trading around $600, the company's management offered to acquire the firm for $14 a share. The bond's conversion value became $507 (36.23 shares × $14 common share price). As with the Caribbean Land Company's example, the price paid for the stock was so low that the conversion value dropped below the market price of the bond. The takeover bid actually caused the price of the convertible to sink.

Even worse, the 6¼ percent Wherehouse bond took on all the characteristics of a junk bond. Management used new debt to finance the buyout, and the older 6¼ percent convertibles became subordinate to it. That is, in the new company's capital structure, the old Wherehouse convertible bonds ranked below the bonds used to finance the buyout. In the vernacular of our times, the Wherehouse bond holders had become "stuck holders." People who owned those converts were outraged. They felt that they had been cheated. Management's buyout maneuver made their bonds convertible, all right, but not for stock—for junk!

It is not hard to argue that the Wherehouse convertibles looked like junk bonds even before the buyout and that anyone who owned them should have known as much. With the Wherehouse stock at $13 a share, the convertible bond holder had to be quite an optimist to put much value in the conversion price of $27.60—more than twice the price of the stock. Besides, at $600, the bond's current yield was 10.4 percent at a time when interest rates of similar-quality bonds were 10 to 11 percent and higher-quality straight debt at 8½ to 9 percent. Convertible securities that trade with large conversion premiums are referred to as *broken, busted,* or even *blasted-out convertibles.* This was clearly one of them. The convert buyers had made an investment mistake. They didn't do their homework. And let's be realistic. If you and I were to engineer a buyout, the smart way for us to do the deal would be to offer to buy the common stock at a price below the conversion price of the convertible securities. Such a maneuver could save tens of millions of dollars because we would not have to pay the convertible holder. In the chess game of smart investing, the buyout guys made a better move than those who chose to hold the bonds.

Wherehouse is not an isolated example of how convertible holders are hurt by buyouts. It has occurred so frequently that most new convertible issues now have *change-of-control provisions* that force the company to buy the convert back at some price higher than the original offering price, in the event of a takeover or leveraged buyout. Not all change-of-control, or so-called friendly put provisions, are the same. (A *put* is a right to sell or put the security back to a company at a set price.) Some friendly puts protect only against *hostile takeovers,* as opposed to friendly ones. A hostile takeover is one the company being taken over does not seek. A friendly takeover is one the company being taken over acts to bring about. Some of these friendly puts have only limited lives; that is, they expire after a certain period of time. The point is, *before you buy a deeply discounted convert, find out if takeover provisions exist and how they work.* And then, read the fine print.

Not all change-of-control provisions are alike. It pays to read them carefully. Kay Jewelers issued high-yield bonds at a time when it had some financial problems, and there were rumors that the company might become a buyout candidate. To protect themselves, should such an event take place, the potential bond buyers wanted a guarantee that if Kay Jewelers should be sold, the bond buyers would be allowed to sell the bonds back to the company for what they had paid, or 100 cents on the dollar, whichever was greater. Kay Jewelers agreed. The general terms of the bond agreement included a clause that the agreement could be modified by anyone who owned more than half of the bonds, although there were some provisions in the agreement, including the interest rate and the interest payment schedule, that were not subject to change. Nowhere was anything written about doing away with the buyback guarantee itself. So, when Ratners Group PLC, Britain's largest jewelry company, offered to buy Kay Jewelers, it offered the bondholders 75 cents on the dollar in order to buy back enough bonds to do away with the buyback guarantee.

The bond holders who bought bonds above $750, especially those who bought the bonds at the initial offering for $1,000, were furious. They felt that Ratners Group had undermined the intent of the guarantee. On the other hand, Ratners Group thought the bondholders didn't have much to complain about. Ratners pointed out that those bonds were trading at $450 to $500 each before their offer was made, and, should the buyout offer fail, these bonds would be likely to trade at those prices again. Ratners maintained that the offer was not only fair but generous.

The rebellious bond holders held out for more. Ratners eventually raised its offer to 90 cents on the dollar, which was about twice the value of the bonds at the time the merger was first announced, and the bondholders sold.

The relationship between a convertible and the underlying common needs continual reevaluation. As the price of each changes, so does the relationship of one to another. The Wherehouse Entertainment bonds did not start out to be junk. When they were first issued, the conversion premium was small. Had the Wherehouse stock appreciated, so would the price of the convertible bond. As the share price fell, the conversion premium became larger and larger. The convertible eventually lost most of its appeal as a stock substitute and began trading like a straight bond, with incidental value being given the conversion privilege.

The lesson is that, as the share price fell, the Wherehouse bond investors should have reviewed their reasons for owning the bonds. If they had bought them as a stock substitute, that reason became less and less valid as the premium grew. Stock-substitute investors should have sold the converts as they might have sold the stock had they owned it instead.

Convertible owners need to ask themselves continually whether they are in the best position. Should they keep the convertible, sell it and buy the common or sell it and avoid the common entirely? Convertibles are not perpetual investments. There comes a time to sell. Be smart enough to recognize it.

Buyout offers generally come without warning. One recent buyout involved a specialty retailer with terrific products and outstanding management whose 7½ percent convertible bonds were convertible at $31.25 a share. At $850, those converts yielded 8.8 percent. The stock was trading in the midtwenties when a corporate raider announced that he had amassed a significant stake in the company and might attempt a takeover. Both the stock and the bonds jumped up in price.

Then came October 13, 1989. The stock market tumbled, and to all the world it looked as though there would never again be a leveraged buyout, including the one involving the specialty retailer. Along with most merger stocks, the common stock of this specialty retailer tumbled from the high twenties to the midteens. The bonds continued to trade in the $850 range, supported by the high return. Even though the stock lost nearly half its value overnight, the converts held up. But the conversion premium had become too large. As the stock fell from the high twenties to the midteens, the conversion premium climbed from 20 percent to 45 percent.

A few months later, when the common struggled into the higher teens, the corporate raider was heard from once again. This time, he offered $23 and, later, $25 a share for the company. The stock shot up to $20 in response, and the bonds collapsed to their $750 conversion value level. The lesson was clear. When the conversion premium widened, the common stock was a better investment than the converts. The higher yield of the converts, in the end, did not justify holding them. The conversion premium was too high. Investors who had bought the converts as an equity substitute should have sold when the premium widened. Pay attention to the conversion premium. As it changes, the convertible must be reevaluated.

When the convertibles tumbled, the bid presented an opportunity for the common shareholders. Because the bond was trading at parity (the takeover conversion value), it made sense to sell the stock and buy the bonds. By doing so, the stock owners turned an investment that was not paying a dividend into an investment that was paying 10 percent ($75 annual interest per bond ÷ $750). If the deal fell apart, they would continue to earn 10 percent on their investment. If the offer were raised, the bonds would go up with the stock. Because the convertible was trading in line with the common, the common shareholder could pick up a 10 percent yield in return for nothing but the transaction costs. Convertibles are to be managed. They work best for investors who are attentive, particularly when events such as mergers and buyouts affect the underlying company.

THE RISK OF DEFAULT

You must decide before you make the investment and while you own the issue whether the company can make its interest payments to you. In other words, what is the risk of default? One way to monitor corporate credit quality is to watch for rating changes.

Each week in its market laboratory column, *Barron's* magazine reports bond rating changes that occurred during the previous week. Upgrades, such as an A rated bond becoming an AA rated bond, are obviously a plus and can positively impact on a bond's price. Downgrades not only have the opposite effect but also can signal a reason to change your decision about investing in a company's convertible. It is certainly a reason to reexamine your investment rationale. In many cases, a downgrade is already reflected in the bond's price. The market has an uncanny ability to be perceptive about "news" that has yet to be printed. Nonetheless, downgrades are not good news and should not be brushed off as nonevents. Ask your broker to help you monitor rating changes that affect the convertibles you own. It is not a bad idea to do a periodic rating review of all the bonds you own. A regularly scheduled bond rating review can help you catch rating downgrades in your portfolio.

You should also read the company's annual report and any research reports written by security analysts about companies you own. Be alert to downgrades of the common stock by securities analysts. Downgrades should cause you to examine why the analyst has become less enthusiastic about the company.

Watch for events that could unfavorably affect the company. (See Figure 4.1.) As an investor, you must always examine the reasons that you own each of your investments. Every investment is bought to be sold at some time. An increased risk of credit quality is one of those times.

FIGURE 4.1   How You Could Lose a Convertible Security

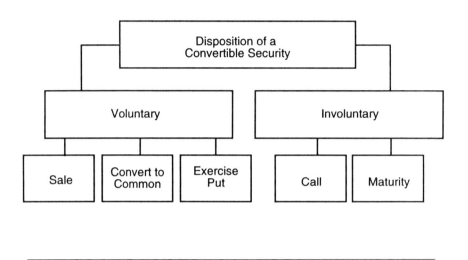

CHAPTER 5

When Convertibles Make Sense and When They Don't

Buying a convertible security for your investment portfolio is a three-step decision process.

1. You should like the prospects of the company in which you intend to invest. As simple as that sounds, if you don't like the company, you should not invest in any of its securities. Big mistakes are made by investors who think of the common stock of a particular company as junk but rationalize that the convertible of the same company, for some reason, is attractive.
2. Evaluate the convertible to determine whether or not it is fairly priced.
3. Decide which is the best way to invest in the company. Is the convertible the best option?

You have trained yourself to ask the question: Is there a convertible security for the company in which you want to invest? You learn that there is. The next step is to decide if the convertible is an attractive investment.

The first measure of attractiveness is *conversion premium*. It is important to know the size of the conversion premium in order to know if the convertible is a bargain or not. The conversion premium is the difference between the convertible's market price and its value if converted into the underlying common stock. We want that difference to be small.

Determining the market price is easy. The Caribbean Land Company 6½s of 02 are trading at 92. We know that the market price of the convertible bond is $920.

Next question. How many common shares is that bond convertible into? Answer: in this instance, 40 shares.

Next question: What is the market price of the shares into which the bond can be converted? Answer: $21.

Next question: What is the conversion value? Answer: The conversion value is $840, $21 (market price of the common shares) × 40 (number of shares into which the bond can be converted) = $840.

Next question: What is the conversion premium? Answer: The conversion premium is $920 – $840 = $80.

$$\$80 \div \$840 = 9.5\%$$

We know that 9.5 percent is considered a small conversion premium. As a result, we should continue to consider the convertible as an investment option. If the conversion premium were larger, we might at this point decide that the convertible is too expensive. *As a general rule, convertible premiums greater than 25 percent are unattractive.*

There may be other considerations. You shouldn't automatically rule out convertible securities with bigger conversion premiums, but 25 percent should be a number that gets your attention. Consider it a warning signal.

IS THERE TOTAL YIELD ADVANTAGE?

The next step in the process is to determine the yield advantage of owning the convertible rather than the common. In our example, we have determined that the convertible is 9.5 percent more expensive to own than the common stock of the same company. A logical question is: Why would we pay nearly 10 percent more to own this security than the common? The answer has to do with how well we get paid as investors to own the convertible versus the common.

We know the convertible pays $65 a year in interest. It is a 6½ percent bond. Assume that the common stock pays a 25-cents-a-year dividend per common share.

With $920 we can buy the bond and earn $65 a year in interest. Our return is 7 percent.

$$\$65 \div \$920 = 7 \text{ percent}$$

Or, with $920 we can buy 44 shares of the common stock. The common stock is trading at $21; $920 ÷ $21 = 44 shares. If we owned 44 shares, our annual income from those shares would be $11.

$$44 \text{ shares} \times \$.25 \text{ dividend} = \$11$$

The income advantage in investing the $920 in one of the convertible bonds, versus 44 shares of the stock, is $54 a year.

$65 (annual interest payment from the bond)
−$11 (annual dividend from the stock)
$54

From an income standpoint, it is clear that we are much better off being invested in the convertible bond than we would be owning the common shares.

BREAKEVEN ANALYSIS

Convertible investors can calculate the amount of time it takes for the convertible's higher yield to make up for the premium paid to buy the convertible security. That calculation is called the *breakeven period. The shorter the breakeven period the better.* In our example the conversion premium is $80. Remember that the convertible bond is $80 more expensive than the shares into which the bond can be converted, multiplied by the market price of those shares. To determine the breakeven period, divide the conversion premium by the yield advantage of the convertible bond.

$80 Conversion premium ÷ $54 Annual advantage of
owning convertible vs. common shares = 1.48 years

The calculation shows that the conversion premium will take 1.48 years to overcome with the higher return from the convertible security. After 1.48 years, the conversion premium will have been paid for with the extra income from the convertible bond. A good rule of thumb concerning breakeven periods is offered by Tony Kreisel, who very successfully managed the Putnam Convertible Income Growth Fund for many years and who now manages the Putnam Equity Income Fund. Tony suggests that breakeven should always occur before the convertible becomes callable. That makes good sense because if a call should prevent you from recovering the premium, the convertible wouldn't have been a wise choice.

THE THREE TESTS

Our convertible security has passed the three critical tests:

1. The conversion premium is small.
2. The income advantage is meaningful.
3. The breakeven period is small.

For these reasons, the convertible security looks like an attractive way to invest in the Caribbean Land Company.

WHEN WOULD THE CONVERTIBLE BE UNATTRACTIVE?

A large conversion premium would make a convertible security unattractive. A general rule is: If the conversion premium is 25 percent or more, the convertible acts less like the stock into which it can be converted and more like an income investment. A lengthy breakeven period is another indicator of a convertible that is more bondlike than stocklike. Convertible investors should want the movement of the stock price to affect the convertible price. The point in owning a convertible security is to benefit from the underlying stock's from going up in value. (See Figure 5.1.)

FIGURE 5.1   Tracking Convertible Security Value

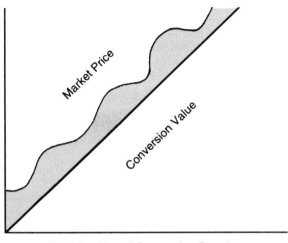

Tracking Size of Conversion Premium

The convertible would also be unattractive if it offered little or no income advantage over investing the same amount of money in the company's common stock.

Figure 5.2 is a Convertible Securities Analysis worksheet. Make copies of it and use it whenever you evaluate a convertible bond or preferred stock. The worksheet provides a quick method of convertible analysis. It won't let you forget the right questions. Don't throw the worksheets away. If you decide to invest in the convertible on which you have done the analysis, the worksheet can be used to keep track of the investment. Consider preparing a simple chart to track the size of the conversion premium. For a callable bond, the chart will help you pay attention to the amount the convertible is trading over its conversion value.

Once a month, you should plot the values to be able to visualize the size of the conversion premium. For a convertible trading above its conversion value, the chart will visually demonstrate its stocklike or bondlike character. As it widens, the convertible loses some of its stocklike characteristics. Pay attention to an expanding conversion

FIGURE 5.2   Convertible Securities Analysis Worksheet

A. Name of company _____

B. Price of common   _____

C. Number of shares into which the convertible
    can be exchanged   _____

D. Conversion value (B – C = Conversion value)   _____

E. Price of the convertible   _____

F. Difference between the price of the convertible
    and the conversion value (E – D)   _____

G. Conversion premium (F ÷ D = Conversion
    premium)   _____

H. Annual income from the convertible (either
    from one bond or one share of the preferred)   _____

I. Annual income from the common into which
    "H" could be converted (annual dividend
    per share multiplied by the number of
    shares into which the convertible can
    be exchanged)   _____

J. Income advantage of the convertible
    (H – I = Income advantage)   _____

K. Breakeven period (G ÷ J = Breakeven period)   _____

L. Price at which convertible is callable   _____

M. Convertible is callable when?   _____

N. Amount convertible is trading over the
    call (E – L)   _____

O. Why did I buy (or not buy) this convertible?   _____

_____

premium. For callable convertibles trading over their conversion value, the chart helps you picture what you stand to lose if the issue is called.

Note also the last question on the worksheet. It asks you to briefly explain your reason for buying (or not buying) the convertible. If that reason no longer applies, perhaps your investment decision should change as well.

CHAPTER 6

Convertibles with a Twist

The convertible security is such a versatile instrument that it has been used by Wall Street's ingenious financial engineers as the basis for myriad innovative securities. Collectively, these "designer" investments are often referred to as derivatives or synthetics. That is because they are derived from more traditional investments or because they have been spliced together from different investments.

The individual investor might be tempted to pass these exotic-looking securities by. Such a reaction would be a mistake because, for investors who do their homework, derivatives can make the most of ever-changing market conditions. Let's take a look at the most frequently used derivatives, beginning with the LYON.

LYONs

A *LYON (Liquid-Yield Option Note)* is a zero-coupon convertible bond. *Zero-coupon* means that it doesn't pay any current interest. A traditional bond, on the other hand, pays a fixed rate of interest—usually semiannually. A LYON, like a U.S. Government Series EE bond, is bought at a discount, and the interest builds up or accrues until the bond matures at face value. The difference between its purchase price—say $400—and maturity value ($1,000) is the interest that has built up over the years that the bond was held by the investor.

Like other convertibles, a LYON can be swapped for a fixed number of common shares. And, in a special wrinkle, LYONs have a valuable put feature that allows the investor to give them back to the issuer at certain intervals, usually every five years.

Here is how they work. The Caribbean Land Company LYONs were issued at $383.09. They mature on December 11, 2004, at $1,000. That works out for an annual accrued, but not paid in cash, interest rate of 6.5 percent. The Caribbean Land Company LYONs were issued when the common stock was trading at $44.75, and they can be converted into Caribbean Land Company shares at $51.463 per share. Each Caribbean Land Company LYON can be converted into 7.44 shares of Caribbean Land Company common stock. At the time of issue, $51.463 − $44.75 = $6.71, $6.71 ÷ $44.75 = 15 percent.

Most LYONs are issued at skimpy (12 to 15 percent) conversion premiums, much smaller than traditional convertible bonds that are usually issued at 25 percent conversion premiums. Remember, the conversion premium equals the difference between the market price of the common stock and the conversion price divided by the market price of the common stock. In this case, the market price was $44.75. The conversion price was $51.463. The difference was $6.71 ($51.463 − $44.75 = $6.71). That difference, divided by the market price of the common, meant a conversion premium of 15 percent ($6.71 ÷ $44.75 = 15 percent).

A small conversion premium is important because it ties the convertible's performances directly to that of the underlying common. Because LYONs pay no current income, they are issued with smaller conversion premiums than traditional convertibles, which usually pay a higher yield than the issuer's common stock. (See Figure 6.1.)

What makes the LYONs most attractive, however, is the put, which is the *investor's right to give the LYON back to the company at a set price at a certain date.* It is almost like owning a stock with a money-back guarantee. Traditional convertibles rarely have put

FIGURE 6.1   Caribbean Land Company LYONs

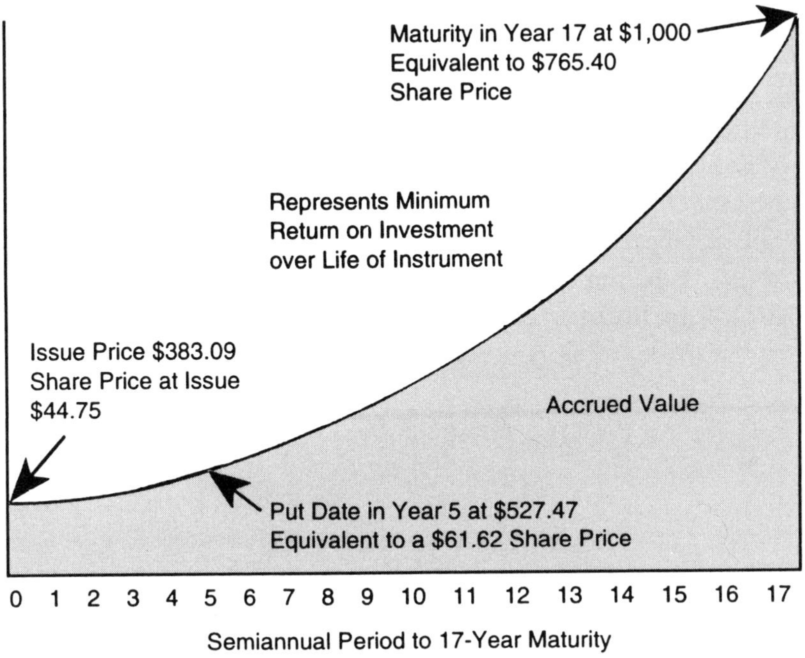

Maturity in Year 17 at $1,000
Equivalent to $765.40
Share Price

Represents Minimum
Return on Investment
over Life of Instrument

Issue Price $383.09
Share Price at Issue
$44.75

Accrued Value

Put Date in Year 5 at $527.47
Equivalent to a $61.62 Share Price

0 1 2 3 4 5 6 7 8 9 10 11 12 13 14 15 16 17

Semiannual Period to 17-Year Maturity

A LYON's value should generally exceed accrued value if the stock price increases sufficiently to cause conversion value to exceed accrued value.

features. In the case of the Caribbean Land Company, the LYON may be put at $527.47, and the put date is December 11, 1994. Assuming the stock appreciates, the investor could not care less about the put because the conversion value of the LYON will be higher than the put price. But if Caribbean Land Company common stock isn't trading above the conversion price of $51.463 on December 11, 1994, the put date, the investor can put or sell the LYON back to the company for $527.47.

That is the worst-case scenario for the LYON investor, assuming the Caribbean Land Company is financially able to honor the put. If the Caribbean Land Company isn't financially able to honor the put, then, as with the securities of any financially troubled company, there is a worse worst-case scenario. But, assuming one owns the LYON of a financially sound company that is able to honor its financial obligations, the investor will be able to sell his or her investment back to the company that issued it at the put price. The put gives a LYON a defensive characteristic not available with traditional convertible securities.

The difference between $383.09 and $527.47, the put price, represents 6½ percent interest compounded over five years. To put that in perspective, the effect of the LYON's rising from $383.09 to $527.47 is the same as stock appreciating from $44.75 to $61.62 a share during the same period of time.

$$\$527.47 - \$383.09 = \$144.38$$

$$\$144.38 \div \$383.09 = 37.69\%$$

$$\$44.75 \times 37.69\% = \$16.87$$

$$\$44.75 + \$16.87 = \$61.62$$

Remember, $61.62 is the least this investment will be worth, assuming it is held to the put date. And if the Caribbean Land Company stock does well, so will the LYON because it is a convertible bond and can be converted into Caribbean Land Company common shares. The put provides the investor with safety of principal and certainty of return. The convertible feature provides the upside potential. That is why LYONs are very popular for investors who want to own common stocks but also want to protect themselves from the risk of losing their investment capital.

Some money managers consider LYONs to be investments with built-in insurance policies. The put feature is the insurance that offers protection against loss. These money managers would prefer to own a company's LYON rather than its common stock because of the downside protection the put provides. Common stocks have no put. These professionals figure that the cost of that insurance is the 15 percent conversion premium. Other money managers argue that the cost is too high and would prefer simply to own the stock. The fact that LYONs exist offers the choice to do either.

A classic example of how a LYON can work for an investor who wants to own a growth stock was the LYON offered by Walt Disney

Corporation. The Disney LYON was guaranteed by the Walt Disney Corporation but convertible into the common stock of Eurodisney Corporation, the European version of Disney World. At the time of the LYON offering, Eurodisney was still under construction near Paris, France. The LYON offering was made two years before the Eurodisney theme park was scheduled for completion. Eurodisney stock was trading at $19.23 a share at the time of the offering, and yet the company hadn't made its first dime. Investors who owned Eurodisney stock were betting on the company's potential. If the Eurodisney park became a success, they hoped their stock would also do well. But the stock offered no downside protection.

The Disney LYONs, on the other hand, were offered at $411.99 each and could be put to Disney on June 27, 1995, at $553.68 each. The LYON investor reasoned that even if the new park never made any money, he or she could do no worse than watch the $411.99 investment increase in price to $553.68. This 34 percent appreciation by the LYONs would have the same effect on an investor's portfolio as would a price move from $19.23 to $25.84 by the Eurodisney stock. Because the LYONs were also convertible into Eurodisney stock at $22.11 a share, if the stock did well, so would the Disney LYON.

As it turned out, the stock did well until the park opened. The day to have sold it for a maximum gain, as it happened, was almost the same day the Eurodisney gates were opened to the public. For a variety of reasons, the Eurodisney share price went into a slump and, owing to their convertible characteristic, the Disney LYONs followed suit. With the Eurodisney stock trading in the $11 to $12 range and the conversion price at $22.11, the LYON's price became a function of the *yield to put value.* That is investors had discounted most of the value of the conversion rights and focused instead on the right to put the LYON at $553.68 on June 27, 1995. Its market price was based on the yield to the put just as the price of a straight bond would be based on yield to maturity. And then came the surprise. The Disney company called the LYON.

Like most convertibles, LYON's have call provisions. Most LYONs offer some call protection for the first two years of their lives, but that protection varies. The Disney LYON was callable at its accreted value. That means that the LYON's yield to its put from its issue price was 6½ percent. At any time after two years from its issuance, the Eurodisney LYON could be called at its issue price plus 6½ percent interest on an annual basis. All convertible buyers, including those who buy LYONs, need to pay attention to call features. Often call protection during the first two years is only provisional. That is, the LYON becomes callable if its underlying common stock trades at a certain price for a certain period of time. For example, a LYON could become callable if its underlying common stock should trade at a certain price for 20 out of 30 consecutive trading days.

After two years, most LYONs, like the Eurodisney LYON, are callable at any time at their accreted value. That means that if a LYON is issued at $350 with a 6½ percent accrued interest rate, at the end of the second year, the LYON can be called at $350 plus two years' accrued interest of 6½ percent a year.

Companies call their convertibles for a variety of reasons. They may be able to issue a new bond at a lower interest rate. A company that is cash-rich may want to pay off some of its debt. Some companies have called LYONs to avoid the potentially heavy financial burden of the put. Others have called their LYONs to eliminate the potential dilution attributable to the underlying shares of stock.

The best way to avoid having a LYON called is to pay attention to both the call price and the conversion value. When the conversion value exceeds the call price by 20 percent or more, a convertible is a likely call candidate. If it is called, the investor will lose that difference because the convertible will immediately trade at its conversion price. The premium will disappear. To maximize your return as a convertible investor, you should always consider how much you stand to lose should your convertible be called. When that amount becomes meaningful to you, and that amount may well be less than 20 percent, switch out of the convertible.

Sell the Common, Buy the LYON or Vice Versa

A strategy employed by some investors who want to give themselves downside protection is to sell the common and buy the LYON, if one exists for the same company.

Motorola issued a LYON in 1990 at $306.50. At that time, the common was trading at $58.37. The LYON is convertible into common stock at $67.125 per share and may be put to Motorola on September 7, 1994, at $411.99. The conversion price was a 15 percent premium to the market price of the common. If you regard selling the bond back to the company on the put date as the worst-case scenario, the net effect on an investor's portfolio would be the same as if the common were to move up from $58.37 to $78.46.

$$\$411.99 - \$306.50 = \$105.49$$

$$\$105.49 \div \$306.50 = 34.44\%$$

$$\$58.37 \times 34.44\% = \$20.09$$

$$\$58.37 + \$20.09 = \$78.46$$

LYON investors are enthusiastic about this investment product because LYONs allow them to invest in a stock they think has great long-term potential, and, even if it doesn't, will guarantee them a profit. If the stock rises above the guaranteed put price, the investors get to enjoy that appreciation as well. A LYON offers those investors a combination of upside potential and downside protection.

Obviously, none of us purchases stocks we think will go down, but every investor knows that some stocks do. Common stocks have no put features to protect investors when that happens. LYONs and other investments with put features allow investors to make some of the inevitable investment mistakes and yet not have to suffer from them. As a LYON supporter might explain it, how well would you have done over your investment lifetime if you simply got your money back for every poor investment you made? A LYON is better than that because it offers better than a money-back guarantee.

There is another opportunity that occasionally presents itself to convertibles investors. It more often comes into play for LYON owners. When a stock collapses, as the stock of the drug company

Alza Corp did, along with nearly all health care companies in early 1993, the Alza LYON didn't decline to the same extent. That was because of the put. While the Alza common stock fell from $46 to $28 (39 percent) the Alza LYON lost only 12 percent of its value. It declined from $330 to $290 (see Figure 6.2). The LYON is putable on December 21, 1995, at $331.41. The yield to the put is 6.4 percent. That is competitive with similar convertibles and is the reason the LYONs, prices declined so little compared to the common.

An Alza LYON investor who really believes in the long-term prospect of the company should use the opportunity presented by this price decline to sell the LYONs and buy the Alza common stock.

One of the oldest and best rules of investing is to *diversify*. LYONs allow an investor to bend that rule. If an investor really likes a company, he or she should feel more comfortable investing in the company's LYON rather than its common shares because of the put feature. Because of this downside protection, LYONs also allow investors to commit more money to an individual company than they might otherwise invest. The overall effect of owning LYONs is that the winners will have a significant impact on portfolios, while the losers will not.

As an investment strategy, not only might it make sense to move money from the common shares of a company that offers a LYON into the LYON, but it also may make sense to move money out of the common shares of a company in the same industry group into a LYON of a company in that industry. For instance, when the Motorola LYONs were issued, some investors not only transferred money from Motorola common into the Motorola LYONs, but from other technology companies into the Motorola LYONs as well. They reasoned that Motorola was a proxy for the technology industry. By owning the Motorola LYON, they could be invested in the industry, but with downside protection. If this concept appeals to you, take a look at the following list of LYONs now available and compare them to the common shares you have of companies in the same industries. Perhaps a swap from the common stock into the LYON is an appropriate way of adding some insurance to your portfolio.

While LYONs are among the most attractive investment vehicles around, be sure you like the company before you invest, just as you do with every other convertible security. It doesn't make any more sense to buy a LYON of a company you don't like than it does any other security. Be sure you also apply the same tests used to evaluate any other convertible. You want to be sure that you are paying a fair price, that you are satisfied with the company's prospects, that the put and call provisions are attractive and that it fits into your overall investment program.

The Negatives

Perhaps the most important disadvantage of owning a LYON is that an investor must pay taxes on interest that he or she doesn't receive. The IRS considers the accrued interest as taxable income. Rather than assuming an equal amount of accrued, or phantom, interest is being earned and therefore is taxable each year, the IRS computes the accreted interest based on a table that assumes less interest earned in the early years of a LYON's life than in the later years.

Because of this taxable implication, LYONs may be particularly appropriate for tax-deferred accounts, such as IRAs (Individual Retirement Accounts), Keogh plans for the self-employed, SEPs (Simplified Employee Pension accounts), corporate pension and profit-sharing plans and some custodian accounts for children established under the Uniform Gifts to Minors Act.

A second important negative is that *LYONs pay no current income,* whereas the company's common may pay a dividend. This characteristic limits the market for LYONs because many investors and most convertible mutual fund managers want some current income from their investments.

The third, and perhaps the biggest negative or source of potential concern, is the put feature itself. As LYONs have grown in popularity, some of the put terms have become less attractive to the investors. Most issuers don't need to honor their puts by paying the investors with cash. At their option, the companies can pay the investors with common stock or straight bonds paying a rate of interest that they themselves have the right to set. Puts of this sort are referred to as *soft puts*. Puts for hard cash, on the other hand are called *hard puts*. A soft put is not necessarily bad but should be understood by investors.

All puts, whether hard or soft, are only as good as the company that must honor them. If the company cannot pay the investor interest when it is due and the principal at maturity, it's not much of an investment, whether it is a traditional convertible, a LYON or a straight bond. This should again remind us of the first rule of convertible investing: Only invest in companies you like as investments, not simply because they are convertible.

Why Companies Issue LYONs

LYONs make sense for the issuer as well as the investor. As a result, since 1985, over $45 billion (face value) of LYONs have been sold. Selling them, like selling any convertible, is the equivalent of selling stock at a premium to the current market price. Remember, most convertible issues eventually are converted into common stock. In the case of Motorola, for example, by selling the LYONs, it was as if the company were selling 52,520,200 common shares at $67.125 instead of the market price of $58.37. The difference between selling 52,520,200 shares at $67.125 a share and $58.37 a share is $459.8 million.

Companies also like to issue LYONs because of the interest savings. Because it is a convertible security, the interest rate that a company will pay on a LYON is much lower than the rate it would need to pay in a straight bond. In addition, because the interest that accrues on a LYON is only paid at the LYON's maturity, the current cash outflow is zero versus whatever the company would need to pay on a traditional bond. That is why the issuing company doesn't have to make any interest payments in cash, yet can deduct the interest expense from current taxes. The amount of money the company saves each year by not paying annual interest, yet receiving the tax deduction, significantly lowers the company's true cost of financing.

FIGURE 6.2   Securities Statistics

SMITH BARNEY CONVERTIBLE RESEARCH
PRICING DATE OF 06/28/93

ALL ZERO-COUPON CONVERTIBLES

SECURITY	CONVERSION RATIO	FIRST CALL DATE	UNLESS COMMON REACHES
ALASKA AIR 0%–4/18/2006	12.396		
ALZA 0%–12/21/2010	8.841		
AMR CORP. 0%–3/15/2006	5.769		
AUTOMATIC DATA PROC 0%–2/20/2012	6.461	02/20/1996	
BAKER HUGHES 0%–5/5/2008	18.599	05/05/1998	
BAROID (VALHI) 0%–10/20/2007	36.077	10/20/1997	14.280
BLOCKBUSTER ENTERTAIN 0%–11/1/2004	27.702		
CHEMICAL WASTE MGT (WM) 0%–4/13/2012	17.218		
CHEMICAL WASTE MGT 0%–8/16/2010	11.676		
COLEMAN (M&F) 0%–5/27/2013	7.853	05/27/1998	
COMCAST 0%–1/15/1995	60.515		
CPC INT'L 0%–6/13/2006	8.114	06/13/1994	75.150
CUC INTERNATIONAL 0%–6/6/1996	101.249		
CUMMINS ENGINE 0%–7/5/2005	4.581		
EASTMAN KODAK 0%–10/15/2011	5.622	10/15/1993	70.725
ELAN CORP 0%–10/16/2012	10.801	10/16/1996	
ENQUIRER/STAR 0%–5/1/1997	36.000	05/01/1997	
FMC CORP 0%–8/7/2011	4.380	08/07/1993	78.540
FREEPORT-MCMORAN COPPER 0%–7/2/2011	15.010	07/02/1993	21.840
FREEPORT-MCMORAN 0%–8/5/2006	13.060	08/05/1993	30.668
GRACE, W.R. 0%–2006–CALLED	8.916	05/16/1993	51.870
HALLIBURTON 0%–3/13/2006	6.823		
HASBRO (TIME WARNER) 0%–12/17/2012	7.301	12/17/1997	
HECLA MINING 0%–6/14/2004	20.824		
LITTON INDUSTRIES 0%–9/26/2010	6.126		
LOEWS 0%–10/17/2004	2.745		
MARRIOTT CORP 0%–6/12/2006	13.277		33.600
MOTOROLA 0%–9/7/2009	9.134		
NEWSCORP (AMERICA) 0%–3/31/2002	15.042	04/01/1995	
NEWSCORP (AMERICA) 0%–3/11/2013	7.113	03/11/1998	
OFFICE DEPOT 0%–12/11/2007	13.006	12/11/1996	
RITE AID 0%–7/24/2006	15.992	07/24/1993	34.650
ROGERS COMMUNICATIONS 0%–5/20/2013	20.675	05/20/1998	
ROGERS COMMUNICATIONS 0%–8/15/2011	19.870	08/15/1993	14.285
RPM 0%–9/30/2012	19.533	09/30/1996	
SEAGRAM 0%–3/5/2006	18.440		
SHONEY'S 0%–4/11/2004	29.349		
SOLECTRON CORP. 0%–5/5/2012	10.396	05/05/1996	
SOUTHERN NE TEL (UT) 0%–2/13/2006	8.358		
SUN MICROSYSTEMS (EK) 0%–9/20/2006	11.702	09/20/1993	43.875
SYSCO CORP. 0%–10/12/2004	24.512		
TELE-COMMUNICATIONS 0%–4/25/2008	16.500		
TIME WARNER 0%–6/22/2013	7.759	06/22/1998	
TURNER BROADCASTING 0%–10/26/2004	15.000		
TURNER BROADCASTING 0%–2/13/2007	12.783	02/13/1995	
US WEST 0%–6/25/2011	6.140	06/25/1993	58.800
USX 0%–8/9/2005	8.207	08/09/1995	57.375
WHIRLPOOL 0%–5/14/2011	7.237	05/14/1993	52.350
WMX TECHNOLOGIES 0%–1/21/2001	34.880		

Source: Reprinted by permission of Smith Barney.

LYON Summary

1. LYONs are zero-coupon bonds issued at a deep discount to face value.
2. LYONs are debt instruments and, therefore, senior to common stock.
3. LYONs are convertible at any time into the issuer's underlying common stock.
4. LYONs are typically issued at a low (12 to 15 percent) initial conversion premium and, therefore, behave more like stocks than bonds.
5. LYONs contain a put provision, allowing the holder to redeem the bonds, thereby providing safety of principal and producing certainty of return, providing that the issuer is financially sound. Either hard or soft put provisions can apply.
6. LYONs can be called. It is important to understand which conditions apply.
7. Interest is not paid periodically but accrues over the life of the bond and can be realized at the put date or at maturity. Interest is taxable in the year in which it accrues, even though it is not paid in cash.
8. LYONs provide protection and opportunity in the case of a takeover.
9. LYONs are liquid because they possess an active secondary market.

PERCs

PERCs (Preferred Equity Redemption Cumulative stocks) are a type of convertible preferred stock that automatically converts into common shares on a mandatory conversion date. This conversion feature provides appreciation potential because the PERC value will increase if the value of the shares of common stock into which it is convertible increases. Coupled with this appreciation potential is a high dividend. Most PERCs pay double the dividend of the under-lying common stock.

One feature that differentiates PERCs from traditional convertible securities is the call price, which serves as an upper limit of a PERC's appreciation potential. Generally the call price is markedly higher than a PERC's original issue price but declines over time until the mandatory call date. And unlike traditional convertible securities, PERCs cannot be converted at the option of the investor.

Here is how PERCs work, using the Sears PERC as an example: Assume that the Sears PERC is priced at $44.75 and convertible into one share of Sears common stock. The common stock is trading at $40.75. The Sears PERC is callable at the time of this writing at $64.25 but that price declines by a few cents each day until the mandatory call date, February 2, 1995. On that date, if Sears common stock is at or exceeds $59, the investor will receive $59 worth of Sears stock. If, for example, the price of Sears common stock were $65, the investor would receive .91 shares of Sears stock (worth $59). That is the upside limit. If the price of one share of Sears were less than $44.75 (the purchase price), the investor would have a loss at mandatory conversion because on that date the PERCs would be worth the value of one share of Sears common. The investor could, of course, continue to hold the Sears common stock and sell it some other time.

The Sears PERC pays a $3.75 dividend, or 8.4 percent. If it were called at $59 on February 2, 1995, an investor's total return would be 24.3 percent a year. That is a combination of the $3.75 dividend per year plus $7.13 appreciation per year ($21.76 ÷ $44.75 = 48.6% ÷ 2 years = 24.3%).

PERCs are, in effect, stocks with generous yields. They offer a trade-off. Investors receive higher dividends than they would if they owned the common stock of the same company. In turn, investors must accept a ceiling on price appreciation. If the common stock does very well, the PERC holder won't benefit beyond the price at which the issuer agrees to redeem it. On the other hand, the higher dividend offers the PERC holder some stability if the common stock trades down.

The concept is identical to the one employed by *option call writers.* To invest in a PERC is not only to acquire an equity but to sell (write) a call option on that equity and to receive some value for selling the call. Like an option, the PERC has a finite life. The higher dividend the PERC investor receives is akin to the income or premium the seller of call options receives from the buyer. What is novel about the concept is that the buyer is the very company that sold the security in the first place.

Most PERCs are originally issued 30 to 40 percent below the redemption price. Most redemption dates are three years from the original date of issue. If the PERCs work as intended, PERC owners stand to make 15 to 20 percent annually over three years.

The drawback is that the higher dividend lasts only until the redemption date, when the PERC is converted into the common stock. If the common's price is below the redemption price, the PERC owner receives a share of common for each PERC, whatever the price of the common happens to be. If the redemption price is greater than the common's price the investor gets a fractional share of the common equal to the value of the redemption price. The formula for calculating the number of common shares to be received is very simple: Divide the redemption value of the PERC by the market price of the common. Let's say the common is trading at \$35, and the mandatory conversion price is \$30. PERC owners will receive .857 shares of common for each PERC owned, \$30 ÷ \$35 = .857. Of course, PERCs trade like other convertible preferred shares in that there is an active market for them. They can easily be bought and sold in the secondary market. In the stock listing table, the PERC is usually listed below the common. It is usually the P series preferred, P of course, standing for PERC.

PERC issuers love to issue them because if their common rises they get to swap fractional shares for each PERC share. If the common were to double the redemption price, the company would be able to pay off the PERC holder with only a half-share of common. Thus, issuers that expect their share price to rise can raise capital by selling fewer shares than they would have to if they simply offered common stock. Assuming the common stock rises above the cap price, the issuance of PERCs lessens the dilution of a company's common stock.

The owner's upside potential is limited by the capped or sliding call price. While the PERC can be called at any time at an

FIGURE 6.3   How the Redemption Cap Works

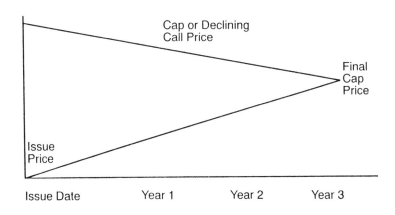

ever-decreasing cap price, the final cap price or redemption price occurs on the mandatory redemption date. (See Figure 6.3.)

Is the PERC a Good Value?

The decision to invest in the PERC rather than the common stock of the same company has to be based on which one you think is a better value. As with any investment decision, you have to like the underlying company. Let's say that you want to invest in RJR Nabisco Holdings and learn that there is an RJR PERC. The RJR common stock is trading at $6 a share and pays no dividend. The RJR PERC trades at $8 and pays a 10.44 percent dividend. The mandatory redemption date is September 16, 1994, and the final cap price is $13.70.

In this instance, if you decided to invest in the RJR PERC simply to earn the high return but didn't expect the stock to rise in value, you would be making a mistake. Although you would earn .835 cents a share for the two years you would own the PERC, on the mandatory conversion date (assuming no price change), the stock you bought at $8 a share would be worth $6 a share. You would have lost everything you earned with the dividend and more. The PERC would only make sense as an investment if its price increased enough to make up for the loss that would occur from the mandatory exchange. If RJR stock were to be at any price above the $8 you paid for the PERC on the mandatory redemption date, it would turn out to be a good investment. That is why you must like the prospects of the underlying issuer, not just the bigger dividend that PERCs offer.

PERCs Can Be Quite Conservative

Take a look at the first Sun America, Inc. PERC. The common is trading at $33.50, well above the mandatory conversion price of 17.55. Think about this. The yield on the PERC is 6.4 percent. The PERC is trading at $17.25, and unless the common falls below $17.55, the investor will receive 6.4 percent and $17.55 for each $17.25 invested. The common would have to tumble 48 percent for an investor to earn less than 6.4 percent annually and essentially get his money back on the mandatory conversion date. As of this writing, similar circumstances exist for the Citicorp, Tenneco and Texas Instruments PERCs. With money market rates in the 3 percent range, these PERCs are worth a look. (See Figure 6.4.)

PERC Summary

Advantages:

1. The PERC holder receives a higher dividend than the common holder.
2. The PERC holder participates to a degree in the upside potential of the common.

Disadvantages:

1. The upside potential is capped.
2. The downside is not.
3. The PERC cannot be converted at the holder's option. The investor would need to sell the PERC and buy the common to

FIGURE 6.4   PERCs

Issue	Dividend	Preferred Price 5/6/93	Current Yield Preferred	Common Price 5/6/93	Mandatory Conversion Date	Conversion Price
Aon Corp.	$3.040	48½	6.3%	54⅝	12/01/94	50.870
Boise Cascade	$1.790	26⅜	6.8%	26⅛	01/15/95	30.880
Citicorp	$1.217	18¾	6.5%	27½	11/30/95	20.28
Consolidated Freight	$1.540	19¾	7.8%	17⅝	03/15/95	30.170
General Motors	$3.310	43⅝	7.4%	40	07/01/94	53.790
Kaiser Aluminum	$0.65	7¼*	9%	7*	06/30/96	10.51
Kaufman & Broad	$1.520	19¼	7.9%	17¼	04/01/96	23.450
K mart	$3.410	47⅝	7.2%	22⅞**	09/15/94	57.200
Olin Corp.	$3.640	46	7.9%	44½	03/01/95	53.950
RJR Nabisco	$0.835	6⅝	12.7%	5⅝	11/15/94	13.700
Sun America Inc.	$1.110	17¼	6.4%	33½	10/15/94	17.550
Sun America Inc.	$2.780	38⅞	7.2%	33½	03/01/96	49.950
Sears Roebuck	$3.750	53⅛	7.1%	53⅜	04/01/95	59.000
Tandy Corp.	$2.140	31½	6.8%	30¼	04/15/95	39.250
Tenneco	$2.800	40½	6.9%	48⅜	12/31/94	42.750
Texas Instruments	$2.260	37¾	6.0%	61	11/01/94	38.740
Westing-house Electric***	$1.530	18¾	8.2%	15¼	09/01/95	23.800

*as of date of issue 6/24/93
**convertible into two shares
***If Westinghouse lacks the funds to pay the accrued dividend at the time the PERC is converted into common, the company must give investors common stock equal to 110% of the dividend in lieu of cash.

exchange the PERC for the common prior to the mandatory redemption date.

4. The PERC can be called at any time.

SIRENs

SIRENs (Step-Up Income Redeemable Equity Notes) are intermediate-term convertible bonds that have two coupons. They pay a below-market interest rate for a few years and then step up to a higher rate until maturity. The blended rate usually ends up being higher than the current going market rate. Investors can convert these bonds at any time. Issuers can call them at the time of the step-up.

SIRENs are ideal for investors who want the opportunity to participate defensively in a company's potential upside. Obviously, if the underlying stock goes up, so will the conversion value of the SIREN. SIRENs are defensive in that investors will be "made whole" at redemption if the stock does not perform well. The worst case would be to have the SIREN called at the step-up date when the stock has not done well. The investor then would have given up a market-rate yield for the period he or she held the SIREN. On the other hand, had the investor held the stock rather than the SIREN, he or she would have lost money during that period. The SIREN at least will return the investment and some interest.

SIRENs work like this. The insurance company Horace Mann issued a SIREN on December 9, 1992. It matures on December 1, 1999. Each $1,000 SIREN is convertible into 28.57 shares of common. At the time the bond was issued, the stock was trading at $26.60. The conversion price was $35. The conversion premium was 23.89 percent. All of this is identical to the characteristics of a typical convertible bond. The differences are that the Horace Mann SIREN pays a 4 percent coupon until January 1, 1994 and a 6½ percent coupon until maturity. The blended yield to maturity from the original offering was 5.79 percent.

Horace Mann and other SIREN issuers are betting that their shares will increase enough so that holders will convert before the step-up. In the meantime, they get the use of cheap money. The SIREN issuer can also deduct the interest expense on the blended rate even though, in the first few years, they aren't paying that rate. An investor must pay taxes on the blended rate even though, in the first few years, he or she isn't earning the full amount.

To obtain this tax benefit, the issuer has to structure the SIREN so that the yield to conversion ends up being higher than the yield to maturity. They do that by putting a fairly healthy call premium on the security. That means for companies to call the bonds they must pay more than they are worth. The premium declines the longer the SIRENs are outstanding so that it disappears at maturity.

SPIDERs

SPIDERs (Standard and Poor's Depository Receipts) are shares of stock that track the performance of the S&P 500. SPIDERs are designed as an index product that allows investors to do as well or poorly as the market. Merrill Lynch marketed two similar products called MITTs (Market Index Target Term Securities), and SMART Notes (Stock Market Annual Reset Term Notes).

A number of banks offer similar investments in the form of certificates of deposit whose interest rates are linked to the performance of stock market indices. The terms of each vary. To avoid surprise, make sure you completely understand how the investment works. The main difference is that your principal in a bank CD is federally insured. The interest is not.

These instruments are for savers who will leave them alone. Most impose stiff penalties for early withdrawal. The brokerage products are liquid. Most trade on the New York Stock Exchange.

LEAPs

LEAPs (Long-Term Equity Anticipation Securities) are long-term stock options. They expire in years, rather than months, as do traditional options. LEAPs allow investors to buy the right to buy

100 shares of a stock at a specific price for a specified time period. For example, a right to buy 100 shares of IBM at $60 a share, expiring in two years, might cost $200. If the price of IBM rises, so will the value of the LEAP. If it falls, so will the price of the LEAP. If IBM is worth less than $60 a share when the option expires, its value will be zero. LEAPs can be traded at any time so that an investor can sell the option rather than hold it until it expires. The advantage of LEAPs over the shorter-term options is that a multiyear period allows an investor to take a longer-term view.

The reason investors use options is for the substantial leverage. One option in our example costs $200, whereas one hundred shares of IBM might cost $5,500. Both represent an identical interest in the price appreciation prospects of IBM. The differences are that the option holder's interest ends at a specific point when the option expires. The stockholder has no such termination date and also gets any dividend that the stock pays.

BOUNDs

BOUNDs (Buy-Write Option Unitary Derivatives) are a type of long-term security that replicates the return an investor would receive from selling (writing) a long-term stock option. Taken together, the price of a LEAP and BOUND should equal the price of the underlying common stock. The BOUND is the income component designed to appeal to more conservative, income-oriented investors who are willing to give up some potential upside in exchange for greater income and reduced risk. The LEAP is the appreciation component.

PAINEWEBBER YIELD DECREASE WARRANT (TURBO WARRANT)

Bets on the direction of interest rates trade like stock on the New York Stock Exchange. *PaineWebber Yield Decrease Warrants* are for investors who want to gamble on an interest rate forecast. These shares increase in value if interest rates decline on long-term government bonds and decrease in value if rates rise. Because they have a relatively short life and can be volatile, they have been dubbed *turbo warrants*, or turbo zeros. They aren't suggested for faint-hearted investors. In fact, most securities firms will require investors to be approved for options trading. The symbol is PYD ws.

SWORDs

SWORDs (*Stock and Warrant Offerings for Research and Development*) or Bio bundles, came about because biotechnology companies need to show earnings to investors, yet need to use whatever they earn to pay for research. To do both, they set up separate companies that sell SWORDs to raise the cash to pay the old company to do research. It is a classic example of off-balance-sheet financing.

Each unit is essentially a combination of two securities. The first is a warrant, or long-term option, giving the investor the right to buy shares in the old company at a specific price for a specified period of time. The second security is a callable common stock. It works like this. The new company pays the old company to do research. The research findings belong to the new company, but if the old company likes the results, it has the right to call the new company's units at a specific price. (After a stipulated period of time the units unbundle and trade separately.) Investors in the units are betting that the research results will be valuable and the units will be called. If the research doesn't pan out, the new company's stock could languish. The rewards can be high, and the risk can be significant. Investments should be made by those who understand what the company is up to and are fully conversant with the terms of the securities.

SYNTHETIC CONVERTIBLES

Anyone can create a convertible by combining a convertible security's two components, growth and income. A *synthetic convertible* differs from a traditional convertible in that it is not one security, but two. Its principal advantage over a traditional convertible is that it can be disassembled by selling one of the components separately.

Synthetic convertibles are most often created by combining a fixed-income and growth component of the same company. The growth component is often a warrant or call option. *Warrants* and *call options,* briefly, are simply rights to buy common stock at specified prices for specified time periods. Warrants generally have longer lives than call options. Both can be volatile, even risky investments—typically moving up or down, in percentage terms, far more dramatically than the underlying common shares. The fixed component is a straight bond. In its simplest form, a synthetic convertible could be a straight IBM bond and some IBM call options.

Because synthetic convertibles comprise two distinct securities with two separate ways of responding to different market conditions, synthetic convertibles will often react differently from ordinary convertible securities. You can package a synthetic convertible in any way you want, like Lincoln Logs, so it is an extraordinarily flexible and imaginative investment. You will notice in Chapter 10 that several fund managers use synthetic convertibles in their convertible portfolios as a means of increasing their "convertible" options.

The most common way of constructing your own synthetic convertible is to buy a straight bond of a company you like. Let's say it is a 10 percent Amazing Growth Company bond trading at $930 for a 10.8 percent yield ($100 annual income ÷ $930 current price of the bond = 10.8 percent). Amazing Growth also has some warrants trading at $5 each. The warrants allow the investor to buy the Amazing Growth common shares at $10 a share. The Amazing Growth common is currently trading at $12.

To determine the number of warrants you should buy, divide the par value of the bond ($1,000) by the exercise price of the warrant

($10). In this example, 100 warrants can be exercised per bond ($1,000 ÷ $20 = 100).

You have built a synthetic convertible by buying one Amazing Growth straight bond at $930 and 100 options at $5, or $500. Total cost is $1,430.

Let's see if your Amazing Growth Company synthetic convertible is a good deal. (See Figure 6.5.)

When you evaluate a synthetic convertible, the key question has to do with the appreciation potential of the warrant, call option or other growth component. You must make a judgment about the potential of the warrant. It's quite simple. If the underlying common shares go up, you win. If they don't, you lose. And because warrants have a limited life, there is a clock ticking away while you wait for your investment to work out.

Figure 6.5 How To Evaluate a Synthetic Convertible

Price of the issue	$1,430
Conversion price	100 shares × $10 = $1,000
Current price of the common	$12
Conversion parity	100 shares × $12 = $1,200
Conversion premium	$1,430 – $1,200 = $230 ÷ $1,430 = 16%
Current yield of convertible	$100 ÷ $1,430 = 7%
Current yield of common	30¢ ÷ $12 = 2.5%
Yield differential	7% – 2.5% = 4.5%
Breakeven period	$230 (conversion premium) ÷ $64.25 (income advantage)* = 3.5 years
Call date	May 15, 1999 at $1,030 (for the bond)
	May 25, 1993 warrant expiration date
Yield to call	the *warrant* expiration is the critical date

*Note: The income advantage was calculated by taking $1,430, the price of the synthetic convertible, and determining how many shares of Amazing Growth Company common that would buy, $1,430 ÷ 12 = 119 shares; 119 shares paying a 30-cent annual dividend produces an annual income of $35.75. The Amazing Growth bond pays $100 a year. The difference ($100 – $35.75 = $64.25) equals the annual income advantage of the bond.

One possible tool to help you evaluate the warrant is the *Value Line Convertible warrant table*, which projects a warrant's potential price change versus the underlying common. It looks like this:

Common + 50% + 25% − 25% − 50%

Warrant + 110% + 50% − 50% − 80%

To calculate the projected percentage move, you multiply the warrant's leverage (i.e., 50 percent) by the amount invested in the warrant. In this example, that amount is $500 ($400 × 50% = $250). Next, divide the $250 by the total cost of the synthetic convertible ($250 ÷ $1,430 = 17.5 percent). According to Value Line's formula, a 25 percent rise in common (from $12 to $16) would result in a 17½ percent rise in our synthetic ($1,430 + $250.25 = $1,680.25).

Those numbers easily work as well for a projected 25 or 50 percent fall in the value of the common. But you really don't need to do the calculations. If you accept Value Line's formula, it is clear that if the common were to move up or down by 25 percent, the effect on the warrant would be identical—up or down 50 percent. If the common were to move up 50 percent, according to Value Line, the warrant in this example would move up 110 percent. If the common were to move down 50 percent, the warrant would move down 80 percent. This looks like a favorable risk/reward ratio.

The Value Line estimates are a useful tool, but, of course, they are only estimates. No one knows what the price of a security is going to be tomorrow, let alone an hour from now.

PIKs

Often a result of mergers, *PIKs (payment-in-kind convertible preferreds)* are commonly referred to as "cram down" securities. That label results from their origin. A company that buys another sometimes pays for its purchase partly in cash and partly with securities that, given a choice, many of the investors would just as soon not own. Those securities are said to have been crammed down their throats. There are now so many of the PIK securities that they have become a significant part of the convertible marketplace. Like every other class of security, some are good and some are not. Being called cram downs doesn't mean that they are intrinsically bad and should be avoided. Again, if you like the underlying company, this investment vehicle may be an ideal way for you to invest in it.

The largest single PIK issue ever was the Time Warner, Inc. convertible exchangeable class D preferred, which, along with the Time Warner convertible exchangeable Class C preferred, was issued to finance the Time, Inc. & Warner Communications, Inc. merger. While they existed, these two securities represented nearly 10 percent of the entire convertible securities market. For that reason, the Time Warner PIKs are a good way to illustrate how PIKs work. Remember the letters *P I K* stand for *payment in kind.* That means that when the dividend is paid, it is not paid in cash, as with traditional dividend or interest paying securities, but rather with more of the same securities.

In the case of the Time Warner convertible exchangeable Class D preferred shares, the dividend payment was made by giving the owners more shares of Time Warner convertible exchangeable Class D preferred on the quarterly dividend payment dates rather than cash. The interest rate for these securities was fixed at 11 percent and the shares were convertible into Time Warner, Inc. common at $225 a share. The term *exchangeable* refers to the right the company has after three years to exchange (at its option) the preferred shares for bonds maturing in 2014 with equivalent interest and conversion features. The shares were not callable until January 10, 1993, unless the common shares traded above $315 a share for 20 out of 30 consecutive trading days. Remember, that kind of call protection is referred to as provisional call protection; that is, the issue can be called *provided that . . .*

In all respects except the term of interest payment, the Time Warner convertible exchangeable Class D preferred shares were like a regular convertible security. Investors who owned these securities were those who liked the underlying company as an investment and wanted a higher return but didn't necessarily need it in the form of cash.

A payment-in-kind dividend is similar to an *automatic dividend reinvestment program.* In a traditional automatic dividend reinvestment program, the cash dividend is immediately used to purchase more shares of the dividend-paying company. In both the automatic dividend investment program and PIK payments, the dividend is taxable in the year in which it is received. Some investors believe erroneously that because they didn't actually receive the cash, the payment is not taxable until they sell the shares purchased with the payment. The IRS takes a different point of view, and theirs is the one that counts. The Time Warner convertible preferred issues turned out to be terrific investments. The Series D issue was called in early 1993. Series C was exchanged for convertible bonds with the same conversion provisions.

CONVERTIBLES WITH RESET PROVISIONS

Another form of convertible security that owes its origin to the merger boom of the 1980s is a convertible with a *reset provision.* The word *reset* refers to the rate of interest the convertible pays. To reset is to raise or lower the rate of interest. Let's say that the Caribbean Land Company bonds due May 1, 2009 have a reset provision. On April 18, 1994, the interest rate of these bonds must be reset to whatever rate it takes to cause the bonds to trade at par ($1,000).

Reset provisions are designed to help the security trade near its face value. Absent other considerations, an interest-bearing security generally moves up and down in price, based on changing interest rates. The idea behind the reset feature is that if the interest paid by the bond were adjusted periodically to reflect changing rates, the bond would behave like a money market fund, and its price would be stable.

The other reasons the price of a security with a reset provision could change have to do with the quality or creditworthiness of the underlying company—and with a convertible security, of course, the price of the underlying common shares.

EURO CONVERTS

Euro converts are convertible bonds traded in U.S. dollars, guaranteed by the parent U.S. company but traded principally in Europe. Companies issue Euro converts when the interest rate they would pay in Europe is lower than the amount they would need to pay in the United States. Companies also do it because the bonds need not be registered with the Securities and Exchange Commission (SEC). That saves time and money. And companies do it because the market for convertible bonds is strong abroad. Ninety days after the Euro converts have been issued, U.S. investors are allowed to buy them. The 90-day waiting period is an SEC rule allowing the bonds to "season." The SEC reasons that because these securities have not been reviewed by the SEC, the trading delay will allow investors time to study the issue and the market time to react to it.

Unlike U.S. converts, nearly all Euro convertibles pay interest annually rather than semiannually. Also, most Euro converts are issued with a shorter maturity than typical U.S. bonds and without a *sinking fund.* Sinking funds are used to retire bonds. Euro bond buyers often require an issuer to obligate itself to repay a certain number of bonds each year before maturity. The reasons are twofold:

1. Bond holders like to see the company reduce its level of debt by buying back its bonds.
2. The possibility of a buyback at par helps to prop up the price of the bonds in an environment where current interest rates are higher than the interest rate the bond carries.

Sinking-fund purchases are at face value ($1,000) or sometimes above face value. Although the European market doesn't insist on sinking funds, many Euro converts have put features.

Historically, European investors have had lousy experiences with high inflation and its effect on bond prices. Many Germans, for instance, can picture older relatives wheeling around wheelbarrows full of near-worthless deutsche marks. Inflation and interest rates go hand in hand. The cost of money rises in periods of high inflation. That cost is reflected in higher interest rates and lower bond prices. European investors have had to confront the pressures of high inflation and high interest rates more than American investors have. They are, therefore, less willing to buy long-term, fixed-interest rate bonds because of having experienced significant price fluctuation in those bonds. The put offers a way for investors to get their money back if interest rates were to rise and the bond price fall.

A telling story about the effects of inflation on bond prices is the one U.S. bond traders told in the late 1970s when the U.S. inflation rate was sky-high, and 8 percent bonds with 20-year and 30-year maturities were selling at 50 cents on the dollar ($500 for a $1,000 bond). "How do you put together a $1 million bond portfolio?" an investor asked. "It's easy," said the bond trader, "Start with $2 million." Although that is hard to envision in the current interest rate environment, believe me, it happened.

A put feature allowing you to sell the bonds back to the company at par or a premium to par can protect you from such interest rate risk.

Euro convertibles trade in the *after market* (after they are initially issued) like any other convertible. Sometimes identifiable by their lower coupon rate and shorter maturity, they also tend to trade with a lower conversion premium and are nearly always issued with a lower conversion premium than new-issue U.S. convertibles. That is another feature European investors expect. These issues are generally more like equities than bonds. Although they are identified in bond guides as Euro converts, you should use the same criteria for investing in one as for selecting any other convertible. Own it if it is the best way to own an interest in the underlying company.

CONVERTIBLES EXCHANGEABLE INTO OTHER THAN THE ISSUER'S COMMON

Some convertibles can be converted into the common of a different company. This situation can result from mergers, name changes, the issuance of securities by subsidiaries or as a means for a company to sell an investment holding.

Evaluating these issues requires two separate analyses on your part. The bond is the debt of the issuing company. You need to be satisfied with the company's creditworthiness. The common stock into which the bond can be exchanged represents the growth potential of the investment. You need to want to own shares of that company. Keep in mind that because you cannot convert into the bond issuer's common, the price rise and fall of the issuer's common is of little consequence (unless its weakness signals a financial problem for the issuer). As you make your investment decision, if the conversion premium is large, the bond issuer should receive most of your attention, because you are evaluating the desirability of the bond as an investment. If the conversion premium is small, the common into which the bond can be exchanged is more important because the common stock is the motive for the investment.

Some convertibles can be converted into common shares plus cash. Some convertible preferreds can be exchanged, at the company's option, into the same company's convertible bonds. Remember the Time Warner convertible preferred Series C example. Forced conversions are generally considered taxable events. For instance, the owners of the Time Warner convertible preferred Series C shares were offered the opportunity to remain invested in the company by exchanging their shares for convertible bonds. The conversion terms were identical but the exchange was considered an *end transaction.* The difference between the value of the shares at the time they were purchased and at the time of the exchange was taxable. It could not be deferred until the bonds were sold.

Because not all convertible issues are straightforward, read every footnote to make certain you understand what you are about to buy.

RULE 144A CONVERTIBLE

Browning-Ferris issued the first convertible ever under Rule 144A, adopted in early 1990. Many other companies have issued convertibles under Rule 144A since that time. The rule allows a company to issue a security in the United States without Securities and Exchange Commission (SEC) review. These securities can only be bought by "qualified institutional investors." This usually means that the institution has $100 million or more under management.

Companies that issue these securities can avoid the time and expense of an SEC review. When a company offers a convertible security but you cannot find where it is trading, that is probably because it is a Rule 144A convertible.

CHAPTER 7

How To Manage Your Convertible Portfolio

"So, when do I convert?" To most new convertible investors, this is probably the most confusing aspect of owning a convertible security. As strange as it may sound, the answer is, "Almost never." This is why.

Let's start with your original decision to invest in the company. Assume that you want to invest in the Morgan Motor Company.

First Question: Is there a Morgan Motor Company convertible issue? You learn that there is. The convertible is a $2.20 convertible preferred stock trading at $31.50 for a 7.0 percent yield.

Second Question: What is the conversion premium? The convertible preferred stock can be exchanged for one share of common at $31.25 a share. The common is trading at $29.63. That means that the conversion premium is 5.5 percent. The conversion premium equals the conversion price minus the market price of the common stock, divided by the market price of the common stock ($31.25 − $29.63 = $1.62 ÷ $29.63 = 5.5 percent). You are aware that a 5.5 percent premium is very small, meaning the convertible preferred shares should move up and down in price very much in line with the common stock.

Third Question: What is the yield of the common? You ask this question to determine if there is a yield advantage to owning the convertible preferred. After all, you are giving up the 5.5 percent conversion premium. The yield advantage is the reason you would do it. If the convertible does not offer enough of a yield advantage, you should buy the common. In this case, the common yields 3.4 percent. The qualitative measure to determine if the yield advantage is great enough is the *breakeven period.* A short breakeven period, whatever the size of the conversion premium, is an attractive feature. The breakeven period simply measures the time required for the convertible yield to offset its premium over conversion value.

Breakeven period = Convertible price
(common price × conversion ratio) ÷ Convertible income
(convertible price common ÷ Common price)

In this example, the convertible yields 7 percent. The common yields 3.4 percent and the break even period is 1.6 years.

Fourth Question: How can it be taken from me? That is, what are the call features? In this case, the Morgan Motor stock is callable now at $31.25. Because the market price is $29.63, the convert would have to rise $1.62 before it would most likely be called. The call in this example isn't a factor. You have very quickly determined that the convertible preferred is an attractive alternative to the common, and so you buy it. Had the convert been trading at too large a conversion premium, or with poor call protection, or with too long a breakeven period, you probably would have decided that the common stock was a better value than the convertible.

Always remind yourself that just because an investment opportunity is a convertible security doesn't automatically make it a better choice. Don't forget the use of convertible securities. Chosen incorrectly, they can be the worst way to invest in a company. Properly selected, they can be among the best. You bought the Morgan Motor convertible for the right reasons.

A few months have gone by since you made your investment. The Morgan Motor Company common stock has moved up from $29.63 to $36. The Morgan Motor convertible has moved up as well, from

$31.25 to $41.00. Because of this price move, the call protection has become an issue. Remember, the convert can be called at $31.25 a share or can be exchanged for one share of common. The convert is now selling at a 14 percent conversion premium ($41 − $36 = $5 ÷ $36 = 14 percent). You realize that if the issue were called, you would lose $5 a share because each of your $41 convertible preferred shares would be converted into a $36 common share.

This is the most important difference between owning a convertible and owning the common. As a convertible owner, you must frequently calculate what you could lose if the issue were called. It is not a difficult or time-consuming calculation, but it is important.

In this example, the convertible you own is trading at $36. The issue is callable at $31.25. If the issue is called, the convertible preferred shares will immediately drop to $36—the value of the common into which it can be converted. It will not drop to $31.25 because it doesn't make any sense to allow the shares to be called at $31.25 when you can convert into a share worth $36. Still, the difference between the current market price of $41 and $36 is $5, or 14 percent. You stand to lose that much if the issue is called.

The income advantage of owning the Morgan Motor convert, while attractive (5.3 percent yield on the convert, 2.8 percent yield on the common—or $1.20 a year more per share from the convert), doesn't seem to be worth the risk of having the issue called and losing $5 a share. Assuming that you still like the company, the prudent investment decision would be to sell the convert and buy the common with the proceeds. You didn't convert the preferred stock into common rather than sell it because the effect of converting would have been the same as if the issue were called. You would have lost $5 a share.

SWITCHING VERSUS CONVERTING

Switching is the sale of what you have and the purchase of what you want. When we sold the Morgan convertible preferred and bought the common, we switched securities. Switching involves commission expenses and tax consequences. Converting involves neither.

WHAT ARE THE TAX CONSEQUENCES?

Be careful! Tax laws change frequently, and you should always check with your tax adviser to make certain of what is current. At the time of this writing, tax rules permit you to go from the convertible into the underlying stock "by their terms" without incurring a tax liability, but not the other way around. "By their terms" has to do with conversion provisions that apply to each specific convertible issue. Tax regulations don't consider conversions to be closed, or final, transactions. The tax liability is, therefore, postponed until the common is sold. The *cost basis* is established when the security is purchased. In our example, the Morgan Motor Car convertible preferred was purchased at $31.25 a share and sold at $41 a share.

If, instead, you had purchased ten convertible bonds for $900 each, total cost $9,000 ($900 per bond × 10 bonds = $9,000), the $9,000 is your cost basis. A year later, you convert the bond into 900 shares of the underlying common. Even though the value of those shares may now be $12,000, under the current tax laws, you pay no tax on the gain. Conversely, if the value upon conversion were less than $9,000, you wouldn't be able to recognize the loss for tax purposes either. Assume the value of the stock into which you had converted the bond continues to rise. Let's say that stock is now worth $15,000, and you sell it. Your cost basis is the original $9,000 that you paid for the convertible bond. Your taxable gain is $6,000 ($15,000 current value − $9,000 cost of the original investment = $6,000 taxable gain).

If the value of the stock had fallen to $5,000, and you sold it, you would have a $4,000 reportable tax loss ($9,000 cost of the original investment − $5,000 current value = $4,000 reportable tax loss).

WASH SALES

There is another tax rule that applies when you sell and then buy a convertible security of the same company. The IRS says that if you do the two transactions within a 30-day period it is considered to be a *wash sale.* A wash sale occurs when substantially similar securities are bought within 30 days before or after a sale that would have otherwise resulted in establishing tax loss. Gains are still taxable. Losses are not deductible. The IRS wants you to be out of a security for at least 30 days, giving enough time for that security to be subjected to market risk, in order for you to count the loss. If, for example, you sold a convertible at a loss and within 30 days bought it back (or the underlying stock or call options or warrants on the underlying stock—simply other ways of owning that stock) you wouldn't be allowed to count the tax loss. The IRS would rule that you hadn't allowed the security enough time to move up and down in price and that you sold it simply to establish the tax loss. To avoid the consequence of a wash sale, you must wait at least 31 days to reestablish your position.

Considering the Morgan Motor car example, you decide to sell the convertible preferred shares and use the proceeds to buy the common shares. Assuming you owned 100 convertible preferred shares, you would receive $4,100, less brokerage commission. Because the commission amount can vary, we will ignore it for the purpose of illustration. But you must certainly take fees into consideration as you make real-life decisions about trading real-life securities. In this illustration, we receive $4,100 and use it to purchase 110 shares of Morgan Motor company common stock.

$$\$4,100 \div \$36 = 110 \text{ (approximately)}$$

CONTINUING TO MANAGE YOUR CONVERTIBLE PORTFOLIO

Let's assume that the Morgan Motor common stock continues to rise. The stock that you bought at $36 a share is now trading at $47 a share.

The company announces that it will issue a convertible bond. The bond will pay 9 percent interest and be convertible into the common stock at $54.05 a share. The conversion premium is 15 percent ($54.05 – $47 = 7.05 ÷ $47 = 15 percent). You consider selling the common and buying the convertible bond. At 15 percent, the conversion premium is reasonable. Checking the call provisions of the new bond, you learn that the bond is callable at $1,030 but that there is hard call protection for two years from the date of issue. Hard call protection means that the bond can't be called for any reason by the company for, in this case, two years. That is also an attractive feature.

At 9 percent interest, the convertible bond is very attractive, versus the common, which, at $54.05 a share, is paying only a 2.1 percent dividend.

$$\text{\$1 Per share dividend} \div \text{\$47 Market price}$$
$$\text{of the common} = 2.1 \text{ percent}$$

Most important, you continue to like the Morgan Motor Company as an investment. You also like the higher income that you would receive from the convertible. You are willing to accept the 15 percent conversion premium in exchange for the income advantage and stability offered by the convert. You decide to sell the common and put that money into the convertible.

There are some pluses and minuses to your decision.

The Pluses

1. Higher income, 9 percent versus 2.2 percent
2. More stability
3. Small conversion premium

The Minuses

1. The 15 percent premium. If you are convinced that the price of the common will continue to rise, why give up a 15 percent premium? The 15 percent conversion premium, while reasonable, is an expensive insurance policy.
2. Assume that the income differential was not significant. Say the convert paid a return only modestly higher than the common

stock. There would then be little incentive to switch. In this example, 9 percent from the convertible versus 2.1 percent from the common stock is a significant yield differential.

3. Assume that the call protection was not as attractive. Instead of the hard call protection, the convert may have offered less desirable soft call protection. In this case, the hard call protection should allow you to participate in most, but not all, of the upside, should the price of the common stock continue to rise.

4. You need to pay transaction costs to make this change. There shouldn't be a commission expense for buying the new convertible issue. That fee is paid by the issuer. There is a commission for selling the common stock.

5. The sale of your common shares is a taxable transaction. You will pay a tax on your gain.

You have just worked through the same investment decision steps while considering selling the Morgan Motor Company common stock and buying the convertible bond that you did when you originally bought the convertible preferred. What should be comforting to you, as a convertible investor, is that the process doesn't change. It is a methodical evaluation to help you determine whether the convertible is a better deal for your investment objectives.

ONE REASON TO CONVERT—MORE INCOME

Common share dividends can increase over time, whereas the income paid on a convertible bond or convertible preferred stock is fixed. It is not unusual for well-managed, highly profitable companies to raise the dividend on the common to a level that is actually higher than the income paid by the same company's convertible. If you own the convertible, that may be the time to convert. But then, it may not be. You will need to consider the yield to maturity and how it may be affected by loss of the conversion premium.

Yield to Maturity.   In the case of a convertible bond, if the bond is trading below par ($1,000), the yield to maturity may be much higher than the current yield of the common. For instance, if the

convertible bond is trading at $880 and pays $45 a year, 5.1 percent
($45 ÷ $880 = 5.1%), and the same amount of money invested in the
common pays 5.5 percent, you must also keep in mind that the bond
will rise to par at maturity; that is, it will increase in value from $880
to $1,000. That gain of $120 per bond is additional income you will
receive by owning the bond rather than the common. In this example,
if the bond were to mature in 10 years, the income pick-up each year
would be $12, added to the $45 annual interest income paid by the
bond, raising the total amount to $57. So the convertible doesn't really
yield 5.1 percent; its yield is really 6.5 percent ($57 ÷ $880 = 6.5%).
That yield is called yield to maturity, as discussed in Chapter 1, and,
in this example, it is clearly higher than the common stock 5.5 percent
dividend return. So, in this example, there is no income advantage to
be gained by converting.

Premiums Should Be Subtracted.   If the convertible bond had
been trading above par, the amount above par—the premium—would
be lost at maturity. Therefore, the yield to maturity would be lower
than the current yield. Say the bond is trading at $1,100 and matures
in ten years. Over the ten-year period, the bond would lose $100 in
value. You would calculate yield to maturity by subtracting the $10
per year the bond would lose over its ten-year remaining life from the
interest payment. If that payment were $45 a year, the yield to maturity
would be figured by subtracting $10 from $45 and dividing that
amount by the market price of the bond ($35 ÷ $1,100 = 3.18% yield
to maturity).

Be careful if the bond is trading at a premium over the call price.
Assume you own a convertible bond trading at $1,150, yielding 4.5
percent and convertible into 100 shares of the underlying common
at $10 a share. The common shares are now trading at $10. Assume
also that the convertible can be called at any time at $1,030.

You are attracted to the hefty 6.2 percent dividend paid by the
common and consider converting to take advantage of the higher
common yield. Wait a minute! If you convert, you will convert into
100 shares trading at 410 or $1,000 worth of common stock ($10 a
share current price × 100 shares = $1,000). You lose $150. Remember, the bond is trading at $1,150. By converting, you lose the

conversion premium, the difference between the investment value of the convertible bond and the market value. Unless the dividend difference is high enough (and in this instance it isn't), it would be a mistake to convert and give up the conversion premium.

In this case, it would probably make sense for you to sell the bond. Because it can be called at any time by the company at $1,030, and its investment value is only $1,000 ($10 per share × 100 shares = $1,000 investment value), if the bond were called, you would lose the difference between the current market price of the bond and the call price ($1,150 − $1,030 = $120). By selling the bond, you could afford to buy 115 shares with the proceeds ($1,150 ÷ $10 = 115 shares) and, because those shares pay a higher dividend, you would increase your return nicely.

THE ISSUE OF QUALITY

Convertible securities have three advantages over their underlying common shares:

1. They offer better downside protection.
2. They offer higher income.
3. By definition, they are of higher quality.

The better downside protection is a function of quality. Be careful not to give up quality for income.

In some cases, the higher dividend is not secure. Dividends can be cut or eliminated entirely. If the company is financially weak, you should be in its strongest security if you are going to own the company at all. Convertible bonds are more secure than common stocks. A good rule is to pay attention to what the market is trying to tell you. If the common dividend is higher than the interest payment of the convertible, the market may be telling you that the dividend is not secure. It may be cut. Rather than automatically assume you have discovered a bargain because of a market inefficiency, check the investment carefully to avoid making the mistake of trading quality for an apparent income advantage.

COMMISSION EXPENSE

Convertible bonds are almost always cheaper to trade than common shares. If you plan to trade out of the issue in the near term, the higher commission expense of trading the common shares versus the bond may outweigh the income advantage.

What Is a Fair Commission?

In the long run, it isn't whether you pay $910 or $920 for the bond, it is whether it goes to $1,300 or $700. Still, every investor wants to know he or she is getting a fair price. With convertible bonds, it isn't always easy to tell because the price often includes a hidden commission. That is because most of the transactions occur in the over-the-counter or dealer market. Even though nearly 75 percent of all convertible bonds are listed on the New York exchange, and many of the rest are listed on the American Bond Exchange, those markets are generally used only for transactions involving ten or fewer bonds. Larger quantities are traded between dealers in the over-the-counter market. For that reason, the prices quoted at the end of the trading day are close to but not necessarily the real market. And the volume shown is a token of what actually traded. For instance, the American Bond Exchange may report that 30 bonds traded on a given day. In reality, 300 of those bonds may have changed hands in the dealer markets. This is not the case for convertible preferreds, which trade either on an exchange or, like a common stock, in the over-the-counter market.

The prices quoted in the newspaper are accurate. This is important to understand because the price at which you may trade a convertible could be different from the one you later see in the newspaper. It may also differ because of the *markup* in the case of a purchase or *markdown* in the case of a sale.

Bond traders make their money from the spreads that exist between *bid* and *ask* prices. A *spread* is the difference between the bid and asked prices. For instance, if a bond is bid $800, someone is willing to pay $800 to buy the bond, and, if offered at $820, some are willing to sell it at $820. The spread is $20 per bond. You will get $800, less commission, if you sell the bond. You will pay $820 plus commission to buy it. Because the spread exists, it always makes sense to ask for a *firm price* before you make your trade. A firm price means the exact price at which you will buy or sell your issue. The price may not be what you expect as it may differ from what you saw in the newspaper. That is why you should ask for a firm price.

Plug the price into the worksheet to see if the idea at the new price still makes sense. If the price is too far away from what you want, you can place a *good till canceled (GTC)* order at a specific price with your broker. GTC orders are offers to buy or sell a security for a certain price. You could, for instance, leave with your broker a GTC order to buy a certain convert at 80 if you are told that it is trading at 82. The GTC order is good for a specified time period, usually 30 days. If the bond trades at 80 or below during the time your GTC order is in force, you should get your order filled. However, if there are orders ahead of yours, you may not. For example, if only five bonds traded and your order was in line behind the five-bond order that was filled, you could read in the newspaper that the bonds traded at 80 but still not be due an execution. Also, GTC orders for bonds that trade only over the counter are not foolproof. Because each broker may trade different quantities of the same bond, it is possible for one firm to trade the bonds at 80 or below and for the firm at which you have your order not to trade any bonds at 80 or below and for you not to get an execution as a result. Still, as imperfect as the system is, it generally works and you should not be dissuaded from using it.

Institutional investors who are trying to trade a large number of bonds generally shop their order with a number of different brokers to get the best price. Shopping orders is like shopping for car tires. You simply call around to find the lowest price. If you are looking for five or ten bonds, it usually isn't worth the trouble because the dealers are unlikely to adjust their prices for small orders. For 50 or more, it almost always is worth the trouble of calling. Often the broker that brought the issue to market (the underwriter) will be able to offer the best price because that firm usually trades the issue regularly or will know where to find the bonds because of familiarity with how those bonds trade.

Back to the example of the convert trading at $800 bid, $820 ask: if you want to buy this bond, you should try to buy it as close to the ask price as you can. Ask your broker for an offering for whatever number of bonds you want to buy. For example, what will it cost to buy 15 of the Morgan Motor 8s of 02 (8 percent bonds maturing in 2002)? Ask if the price quoted includes the commission. If it does, and the price is higher than the ask price, either the market is strong and the price is rising or the price difference is the commission.

One of the silliest mistakes convertible investors make is to miss a good investment rather than pay a few more dollars than they would like. But one of the dumbest mistakes is to pay too much unnecessarily. If the price quoted to you seems high and there aren't good reasons for the convertible's price to be moving up—such as the underlying common moving higher or interest rates falling— leave a GTC offer with your broker and see if you get it at your price. He or she may be able to fill your order by reducing the commission or by negotiating with the seller.

WHAT IS A FAIR PRICE?

When you are buying a convertible bond, the best price is the bid plus as small a markup as possible. When you are selling, it is the offer less as small a markdown as you can get. In the real world, for ten or fewer bonds, that difference ideally shouldn't be much more than $10 a bond; for larger quantities it should be less.

Whatever the price, when you are evaluating a purchase be sure that when you do the calculations that the numbers, including the commission, make sense. If the markup and/or commission make the yield significantly less attractive or materially affect the break-even period or make the call price a bigger factor, the investment may not be as attractive and perhaps should be avoided.

YOU NEEDN'T CONVERT TO SELL

Another misconception of many new convertible investors is a belief that they must convert into common shares in order to get out of their convertible investment. Not true. Convertibles can be sold just as they can be purchased—as convertible securities. They needn't be converted into the underlying common shares to be sold.

YOU WILL EARN INTEREST UNTIL SETTLEMENT

Assume that you decide to sell the Morgan 9 percent converts. Assume also that they pay interest semiannually, on January 1 and July 1 of every year, and that you sell the bond on October 12. Interest accrues on all bonds on a 360-day calendar because Wall Street recognizes only 360 days in a year for interest calculations. You earn interest for every day you own a bond. In this case, the last interest payment you received was on July 1. When you sell the bond, you are entitled to the interest that has accrued from July 1 through the date of your sale, October 12. On ten bonds, that amount is $225. It is calculated as follows: At 9 percent interest, ten bonds pay $90 a year or $900. The daily rate of interest earned is $900 ÷ 360 days = $2.50 a day. From July 1 through October 12 is 102 days; 102 days × $2.50 = $225 accrued interest. This is exactly how accrued interest is calculated for every bond. Convertible bonds differ in one important way: *If you convert into the common stock, you lose the accrued interest from the last payment date.*

Convertible preferred stocks usually pay quarterly dividends like common stocks. And, like common stocks, they need only be owned by the investor on the dividend record date to earn the quarterly dividend. Unlike a bond, the income doesn't accrue. Whoever owns the convertible preferred on the dividend record date is entitled to the entire quarterly dividend. That is why you should always *check the record date before selling.* It is silly to miss a dividend payment simply by inattention. You can check the date with your broker or by reading any stock guide.

CUMULATIVE IS A VALUABLE PROVISION

Most preferred stocks are cumulative preferred stocks. In the newspaper, the abbreviation for the term is cm. A Caribbean Land Company $3.00 convertible cumulative series A preferred would be listed as

Caribbean Land Co 3.00 cv, cm pr A.

The term cumulative means that if the Caribbean Land Company skipped any preferred dividend payments those payments would continue to accumulate and be owed to whoever owned the preferred stock when the company is able to pay those dividends. The debt doesn't disappear just because the company isn't able to pay it on the dividend payment date. Generally the company is not allowed to pay any dividend on its common stock until all of the cumulative preferred dividends in arrears are paid.

Remember that the dividend is payable to whoever owns the preferred at the time the company is able to make the payment. That means you could buy the cumulative preferred of a company today and receive several years' worth of back dividends a month from now simply because you own the stock when the company is able to repay its back dividends.

My first experience with this type of preferred stock was Chrysler Corporation. When it turned around financially and was able to pay its back dividends, the owners of Chrysler Cumulative convertible preferred did well indeed. Subsequently, International Harvester, Gulf States Utilities and MNC Corporation Cumulative preferred shareholders have benefitted from the same kind of financial turn-around. These types of situations exist. For investors who are willing to take the risk that a financial turnaround will occur, big payoffs are possible. Where can you find these preferreds? Simple, get a copy of the S&P monthly stock guide. Look through the book at the column on the far right of the odd-numbered pages. The column is titled "Interim Earnings." Dividends in arrears are noted as follows: Accum $4.50 to 4-15-93. This means that this particular preferred is $4.50 in arrears through April 15, 1993.

WHAT IF THE PRICE OF THE COMMON BEGINS TO FALL?

Let's say you own the Morgan Motor Car common stock and for some reason—poor earnings, poor business prospects, poor economic environment or even a weak stock market—the Morgan Motor Car common stock begins to slide. You know that there is a Morgan convertible bond and you are considering selling the common and putting that money in the convertible. You are thinking about doing that because even though you are somewhat less certain about the prospects of Morgan Motor Car Company, you feel an allegiance to a stock that in the past has treated you well. Is this a good idea? Probably not. *A convertible shouldn't be used as a substitute for a bad investment.* If the common stock is a poor investment, the convertible security of the same company will also likely be a poor investment. That is because a weak common stock price will drag the price of the convertible down with it. As the common stock price falls, the conversion premium will grow, and the bond will lose its stock-substitute characteristic. When that happens, the income that the convertible pays will become the convertible's principal attraction as an investment. Convertibles generally don't make sense as common stock investment substitutes to be used to ride out hard times in weak companies. Better advice is to avoid any investment in the company.

WHAT IF THE SHARE PRICE DECLINES, AND YOU DECIDE TO HOLD?

Assume the price of the Morgan Motor Car common declines and you hold it. Watch the conversion premium! As the stock price falls, the conversion premium will grow. As it grows, the convertible loses its stock-substitute characteristics. That is because the convertible's price will be less affected by the price movement of the underlying common shares.

As the conversion premium increases, you must decide on your motive for investing in the Morgan Motor Company. If it is to benefit from the price movement of the common stock, you should sell the convertible and use the proceeds to buy Morgan common shares. If you don't do that and continue to hold the convert, you will find that it has lost its stock-like characteristics and behaves more like a bond—its price changing with interest rates rather than with the prospects of the company. If you have held it, you are no longer in the investment for the reason you intended. That is almost always a prescription for disaster. Don't rationalize a lousy investment. Get Out!

WHAT IF THE CONVERT SIMPLY STALLS?

Let's say the market price of the Morgan convert doesn't seem to want to go up or go down. The market in general is flat and you consider selling call options against your Morgan convert.

Call Options Defined

A *call option* is the right to buy 100 shares of a common stock at a certain price for a certain period of time. The right to buy 100 shares of Morgan Motor at $50 a share until the third Friday at 3:00 pm on July of next year is an example. Most call options trade on organized option exchanges such as the Chicago Board of Options Exchange (CBOE) and have expiration dates that are the third Friday of a given month.

The call option itself is a security that trades on an exchange, just as the common shares trade on an exchange. The price of that option will go up and down with the price of Morgan Motor stock. If, for instance, Morgan common is trading at $55 a share, the call option will trade at least at $5 a share, the difference between the price at which the option can be exercised—$50—and the market price of the stock ($55 – $50 = $5). That price is referred to as the options' intrinsic value. Depending on how much time between now and July when that call option will be higher than $5 reflecting the time value and its potential during that time to go higher in price than $55. The price of a call option is a combination of its intrinsic value ($55 –

$50 = $5), plus its time value. The closer to July, the smaller the time value of the call option because there is less potential for the stock to go higher in price in a shorter period of time than in a longer period of time.

Investors who own 100 shares of Morgan Motor or any stock on which call options are traded can sell an option on their stock and collect the premium for doing so. Let's say it's $7 and the seller of the option guarantees that he or she will give his 100 shares of Morgan Motor to the buyer of the option at $50 a share at any time until the option expires.

You can readily see that if the price of Morgan Motor common stock drops below $50, the investor who owns the stock won't need to give up those shares. If it is above $50, he or she can either deliver the shares to the buyer at $50 each or buy the option back and keep the shares. If Morgan Motor stock is at $59, for instance, the call option will be trading at least at $9. Buying it back will result in a loss of $2 ($9 buyback price – $7 original sales price = $2 loss).

Investors sell call options to increase their return from their investment. What does this have to do with the Morgan Convertible? Convertible owners can do the same. It works this way. Assume the five 9 percent Morgan convertible bonds can be converted at $50 a share. Assume further that the Morgan Motor common is trading at $55 a share. According to the options tables in the financial press, options on the Morgan common are trading for several time periods at prices ranging from $55 to $65 a share. Options usually expire quarterly and are traded in $5 or $10 increments, based on the price of the common stock. (See Figure 7.1 for the Morgan Motor option's prices.)

Option prices are quoted in fractions just as common stock prices. Reading across the top line, the $55 call option expiring in April closed trading the day before at $5; the July $55 option closed at $7.50, and the October $55 (as it is called) at $9. Because all options sold are for lots of 100 shares, $5 per share means $500 for 100 shares, $7.50 per share means $750 for 100 shares, and so on.

Because each of our Morgan bonds is convertible into 20 shares, or a total of 100 shares at $55 a share, we could sell the $60 July option and earn a $500 premium for each five bonds we own.

FIGURE 7.1   Morgan Motor Option's Prices

Option's Price	Expiration Months		
	April	July	October
55	5	7½	9
60	2½	5	6½
65	1¼	3⅞	4¼

By selling the call option, we've agreed to deliver 100 shares of the common if the option is called anytime between the time we sell the option and when it expires. In exchange, we are paid the option premium of $500 at the time we sell the option.

Our motive for selling, or *writing the option* (as it is called), is to try to increase total return. We know that the convertible will pay $450 interest over the year (9 percent × $5,000), but the additional $500 option premium income will boost our return to 19 percent ($450 + $500 = $900 ÷ $5,000 = 19%). Further, if the underlying Morgan Motor stock moves up from $55 to $60 a share, the investment value of the bond will increase from $1,100 to $1,200 (20 shares × $55 per share =$1,100, 20 shares × $60 per share = $1,200). That additional $100 would increase our total return even if the option were exercised to 21 percent ($450 income + $500 option premium + $100 bond investment value increase = $1,050 ÷ $5,000 = 21%).

As an option writer, we give up any appreciation of the Morgan Motor common over the option exercise or strike price. Having sold the right to someone to buy it from us at $60 means that we obviously won't benefit from any price increase above $60—even if the underlying common were on a romp to $70 a share. But wait a minute! With a convertible, that isn't entirely true—because the investment value of the bond will increase from $1,200 to $1,400 if the underlying common moves from $60 to $70 (20 shares × $60 = $1,200, 20 shares × $70 = $1,400). There will also presumably be some premium on the bond because of its income. So, rather than convert, we could sell the bond, buy common on the market at $70 to deliver to the option buyer and keep the difference.

The best time to sell options against the convertible securities, or against common stock for that matter, is when you expect the price of the common to remain flat. It would be silly to sell call options against a security that you expect to appreciate during the time the option is outstanding because by selling the call option you would give up that appreciation. It also makes little sense to sell call options against a security that you expect will soon fall in value. Unless the price decline is expected to be short-lived (and who knows?), it is better simply to get out of the security entirely.

Option writing can add value to the management of your portfolio and there are numerous strategies. The one just illustrated is the most typical. Another has to do with convertibles that are likely call candidates.

If you want to protect yourself from losing the premium over the market price of your convertible you can sell call options against your convertible. By selling the call options you may be able to raise enough cash to make up for some or all of what you would lose if the convertible is called. This is what I mean. Assume that the Morgan Motor convertible is trading at $1,400. It is convertible into 20 shares of Morgan Motor common, which is trading at $65 a share. The conversion value is $1,300 (20 shares × $65 = $1,300). You stand to lose $100 per bond if the convertible is called ($1,400 market price − $1,300 conversion price = $100). You own five bonds. Because each is convertible into 20 shares, you have the conversion rights to 100 shares. By selling the $65 July call options, you will receive $500. Now if the bonds are called, you will lose the market premium of $500, which you already earned by selling the call options.

USING MARGIN TO BUY CONVERTS

You borrow money to invest if you think you can earn more with it than it cost to borrow. Borrowing provides leverage. Leverage is simply the effect of having more money in an investment than you might otherwise have. It magnifies investment results, both good and bad. Brokerage firms will lend you money based on the value of your securities. The term *margin* has to do with the securities held by the brokerage firm as collateral for the loan. The size of the loan that is permissible is determined by the brokerage firm, the stock exchange and the Federal Reserve Board, and it changes from time to time, based on regulatory changes.

It works like this. You have enough cash to buy 25 of the new Morgan 9 percent converts, but you want to buy 50 or $50,000 full value. You pay $25,000 toward the purchase, leaving yourself with a $25,000 debit balance. A debit balance is the amount you owe the brokerage firm, for which you will be charged interest. Assuming the interest rate is 12 percent, the loan will cost you $8.33 a day ($25,000 × 12 percent = $3,000 ÷ 360 days = $8.33 a day). A 360-day calendar is used to calculate interest charged to borrow money just as it is to calculate interest earned on bonds. Because the bond pays 9 percent interest, you are earning $12.50 a day ($50,000 × 8 percent = $4,500 ÷ 360 days = $12.50 a day). Should the bond appreciate from $1,000 to $1,050, you have made good use of leverage. The $25,000 you invested would have appreciated by $2,500 ($52,500 – $50,000 = $2,500) or 10 percent ($2,500 earned ÷ $25,000 invested). In addition, you have been earning $4.17 a day interest ($12.50 – $8.33 = $4.17 = 6 percent a day ($4.17 × 360 days = $1,501.20 a year ÷ $25,000 = 6% interest)).

The risk is that the bond loses value while you are borrowing money to buy it. Should it drop from $1,000 to $950, just as leverage can magnify your gain, it can magnify your loss. Instead of being worth the $25,000 you invested, your account would be worth $22,500. The value of your holding would have shrunk from $50,000 to $47,500, while the debit balance remains $25,000, the amount you borrowed to make the purchase.

If the price of the convertible should fall far enough, you would be forced either to add money to your account or sell some bonds. That is referred to as a *margin call*.

Margin can work for you, helping you build your capital by shrewdly using someone else's money. Margin can also work against you because you stand a chance of not only losing your money but money you borrowed as well. Using margin is clearly not for every investor. There is the risk that what you have borrowed to buy will decline in value, and there is the risk that the rate of interest you are charged to be on margin will increase, possibly wiping out any income advantage. If that happens, you will be paying more to borrow the money than your investment is earning. Margin interest rates fluctuate with short-term interest rates, having no ceiling or floor. The example showed a positive interest rate carry ($12.50 earned versus $8.33 charged). Should rates rise, that could disappear or become negative. The interest charged becomes part of your debit balance, and you will pay interest to borrow it as well. Payments made into your margin account reduce the debit balance.

THE CONTINUAL SEARCH FOR WAYS TO BETTER YOUR POSITION

Managing your investments, including your convertible securities, should be a continual search for ways to better your overall investment position. Each security you own is a commitment of a certain amount of money. That amount shouldn't be thought of as what it was when the investment was made but what it is now. That, after all, is what it is. After you come to grips with that fact, the follow-up question has to do with how smart an investment commitment it is.

If you can improve it, do it! Convertible investing can't be done well by inattentive investors. Convertible investors must be vigilant. Prices change. The risk of a call can come into play. The yield or growth advantage may shift from the convertible to another security. The financial position of the company or the price action of the underlying common may change. You must stay alert to all these changes and make changes yourself, when appropriate, to better your position.

CHAPTER 8

How To Identify Good Convertible Ideas

A good convertible idea is always a byproduct of a good investment idea. If you don't think much of a company, regardless of how attractive the convertible might appear, it almost always isn't a good investment. The first hurdle a convertible investment idea must clear is that you believe in the investment potential of the underlying company. Having made that point, it is important to acknowledge that there are occasions when a convertible security is so attractive that its attractiveness becomes the reason you want to own it.

The Time Warner Convertible preferred Series D PIKs are an example. As was earlier pointed out, these securities no longer exist. They were called in early 1993. However, there was a time that these shares were priced to yield over 12 percent. The conversion premium was sky-high, so they didn't make sense as a stock substitute. But, for a variety of reasons, they appeared to make sense as an investment. The company appeared to be doing all of the things it could to pay off its monstrous debt resulting from the merger of Time, Inc., and Warner Communications. The PIK seemed to be a logical candidate for redemption because it was the type of high-cost debt Time Warner publicly stated that it wanted to do away with. And it turned out that way. Investors who bought these securities when they were priced to yield 12 percent and considered to be a junk security by many did very well. Where did they get the idea?

One source of convertible ideas is to find out what the convertible professionals own and are buying. You can do that by reading the quarterly reports of convertible mutual funds. Each is required to list the holdings. By reviewing the list, you may uncover convertibles that you didn't know existed. The performance record of the convertible fund manager is public information. Look at what the better managers own and are buying. It may be just as important to pay attention to what the better managers have sold.

Michael S. Rosen is the manager of the Bond Fund for Growth, formerly the Rochester Convertible Fund. This fund was the top-ranked convertible fund in 1992 by Lipper Analytical Services Inc. And in the December 28, 1992, issue of *Business Week,* Michael was named the top bond fund manager for 1992. He points out that convertible ideas fall in four main categories:

1. *Traditional Convertibles* have 20 to 30 percent conversion premiums that yield 2 to 4 percent less than nonconvertible debt of similar quality.
2. *Broken Convertibles* (the category the Time Warner converts would have fallen into) have large conversion premiums and high yields. These investments involve more risk and require greater analysis but it is often where great bargains exist.
3. *Short Effective Maturity Convertibles* have either short stated maturities or puts. The common stock may not be exciting, but the combination of potential upside and downside protection offered by the short life make the investment worth considering.
4. *Equity Substitute Convertibles* have very small conversion premiums, yet, because of their higher yield, offer a distinct advantage over the common shares.

Good convertible ideas can be found in all of these categories.

Not only do the quarterly reports tell what the fund owns but the price at which those converts were bought. From that information, you can make a judgment about whether you may be too late. That is, the price the fund paid may be considerably less than the current market price. At its current price it may not be a good value. Check each of the ideas that appeal to you by finding a current price. That can be easily done by looking at the convertible securities listing in

Investors Business Daily or by calling your broker. The price will also be listed in *The Wall Street Journal*, although the *Journal* doesn't list convertibles separately. You will have to look through the various bond and preferred tables.

The Morningstar Mutual Funds, published biweekly by Morningstar, Inc., 53 West Jackson Boulevard, Chicago, IL 60604 ($395 a year), also lists the largest holdings of each convertible fund. Figure 8.1 shows a sample Morningstar report. The box in the lower right-hand corner lists the convertible holdings of the Calamos Convertible mutual fund. It is useful to study because it offers so many ideas. For instance, you may be interested in Ford Motor Company as an investment but unaware there is a Ford Motor Convertible. Or you may not have considered Wendy's International but, now that you know that there is a Wendy's convertible bond, you may want to consider the idea further.

Look under the analysis section. It gives you an idea about the Calamos Investment Strategy. Perhaps that makes sense to you, and you may decide to implement it for yourself. The total return section tells you how well the fund has done during the last six years.

The more time you spend studying the Morningstar report, the more helpful you will find it can be. Morningstar is available at many libraries and probably through your stock broker.

Ask your broker for a copy of Standard & Poor's stock and bond guides. These monthly publications provide thorough information about convertibles. There is a separate listing in the back of the bond guide for convertible bonds. Convertible preferreds are listed in the stock guide following the common. For example, the Ford Motor Company common stock is the first listing for Ford in the stock guide. The convertible preferred follows.

Ask your broker to find out what the wrap account convertible managers are buying. *Wrap accounts* are professionally managed brokerage accounts for which an investor pays a management, or wrap, fee but no brokerage commissions. There are wrap managers who specialize in convertible accounts. By looking at what they are buying, holding and selling, you can get some more ideas. Keep in mind that professional money managers make investment mistakes like everyone else. Lists of their holdings are simply sources of ideas from which you can start your evaluation process. These lists are not endorsements for fail-safe investments. Ideas for investments come from an unlimited number of sources. One of the best, it is hoped, is your broker or financial adviser. Make certain that he or she understands that you are interested in convertible securities. Most brokerage firms publish reports on convertibles. You should be on your broker's list to receive them. Many securities firms also include in their research reports about particular companies, information about that company's convertible securities, if any exist.

The *Value Line Convertibles Report* and the *RHM Convertible Survey* (both referred to in Chapter 2) are excellent guides for convertible investors.

FIGURE 8.1   Example of Morningstar Report

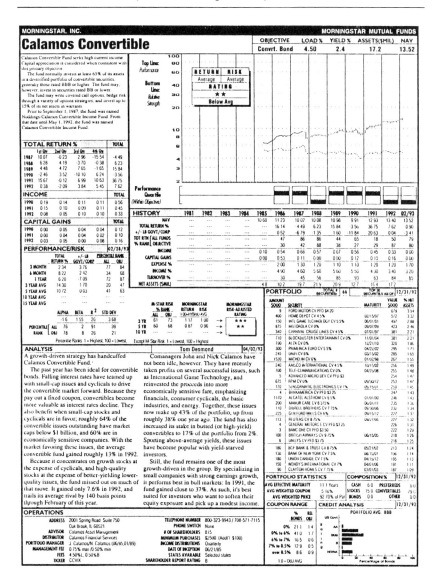

CHAPTER 9

Where Convertibles Fit into Your Investment Portfolio

Convertibles fit into both the stock and bond portions of your portfolio, depending on their conversion premium. Those with large premiums count as bond substitutes. Those with smaller premiums act more like common stocks and should be counted in the equity portion of your portfolio. The principal rule that investors should observe in constructing a portfolio is to strive for balance. Your investments should be spread among a wide variety of stocks, bonds, convertibles, real estate, cash alternatives and global securities.

A balanced portfolio includes a mix of investments that respond differently to differing market conditions. A great deal of attention has been paid lately to *asset allocation*, which simply means dividing your investment portfolio among different classes of assets. Asset allocators argue that performance has more to do with being in the right asset class at a particular time than investing in the individual investments within the asset class. For example, it is more important to have a large portion of your investments in bonds than in any particular bond when the bond market is strong.

Just how much of your assets you allocate to different investment classes has to do with how comfortable you are with the particular class. Making investors more comfortable is precisely the advantage of convertible securities. Convertibles offer the opportunity for growth along with a comparatively attractive stream of income.

Conservative investors can choose among the convertibles offered by high-quality companies. Because of their downside protection, LYONs are also ideal for risk-averse investors. Investors who are willing to take somewhat greater risks can include in their portfolios convertible securities of lesser-known companies with strong growth prospects. Aggressive investors can select convertibles that others may have mistakenly categorized as junk or have overlooked. Remember, many convertibles have been issued by small companies that are too obscure to attract institutional interest or Wall Street research coverage. There are bargains among convertibles for those willing to do their homework.

GROWTH IS IMPORTANT FOR EVERY INVESTOR

When economists use the word inflation, they are talking about a concept we all understand. It doesn't take a degree in economics to be aware that nearly everything we buy and every service we use costs more money this year than it did last year. So it just isn't enough for us to preserve capital. We have to find ways to make our investments grow so that our money will keep up with ever-escalating prices.

That means it isn't enough for investors to park money only in fixed-income securities such as Treasury bills, money market funds or straight bonds and expect the portfolio to stay even with the cost of living. Inflation prevents that from happening. Some part of every investor's portfolio, regardless of an investor's age, must provide growth. It is wrong to assume that older investors should have nearly all of their money in bonds. It is equally wrong for younger investors to have all of their investable dollars in high-flying growth stocks. Older people, some advisers reason, can't replace any money they lose, so they shouldn't subject what they have to risk. Younger investors can replace what they lose so they should be aggressive.

No one should invest to lose money. Investments should be made as part of a portfolio that provides enough diversification to minimize the impact of poor choices. Your portfolio should be managed carefully rather than left untended.

Over time, investments in well-chosen common stocks and convertible securities should provide the growth every investor needs to battle the effects of inflation. That is why they should be part of every investor's portfolio.

A CASE FOR EQUITIES

Starting in 1925, one of the boom years leading to the 1929 Wall Street crash until the end of 1991, common stocks outperformed Treasury securities by a wide margin. A hypothetical investment of $1,000 in 1925 in common stocks with dividends reinvested would have been worth $727,380 at the end of 1991. Had the investor spent the dividends, the $1,000 would have grown only to $41,600. This shows just how significant the dividend portion of one's investment can be. This is another argument for convertible securities and the high income they provide. The same $1,000 invested in U.S. Treasury bills (bills are the shortest-term government investments, with maturities that are either 90, 180 or 360 days) would have grown to $11,400 *with all interest reinvested.* One dollar invested in Treasury bonds (maturities from 1 to 30 years) would be worth $23,710 with all interest reinvested.

Common stocks outperformed Treasury bills and bonds in nearly all holding periods of 1, 5, 10 and 15 years that can be constructed during those 66 years. Although the past isn't a guarantee of the future, the historical results are a strong argument that the apparent safety of investing entirely in fixed-income securities isn't all some investors assume it's cracked up to be.

DIVERSIFY YOUR INVESTMENTS

If nothing else became clear to investors during the past half-dozen turbulent years—years that produced stock and bond market activity that is likely to be studied by succeeding generations—it was the need for investors to diversify their investments. That doesn't just mean diversifying among various stocks or bonds, or owning certificates of deposit that mature on different dates. It means allocating your investable assets among different asset classes such as stocks, bonds, money market investments and real estate, and within those classes, among unrelated securities and among different maturities. Common sense dictates that while diversification should be adequate, it shouldn't be so excessive that you can't keep track of what you own. As far as stocks and bonds are concerned, most individual investors would do well to own

- few enough so that each has an impact on your portfolio;
- few enough so that your best ideas are not diluted by your twentieth best idea;
- few enough so that you understand each very well.

Each of your positions should be unrelated to the rest. It's wise to keep your money in a manageable number of attractive situations and then watch them closely. Ideally, you want events affecting your securities to sneak by you as easily as it is to sneak sunrise past a rooster. That certainly doesn't mean you can't follow another 30 or 40 companies and learn to understand them as well, but you don't have to own every company you follow.

STAY ON TOP OF YOUR INVESTMENTS

There is an investment club that owns only as many stocks as it has members. That is because each member is responsible for monitoring one stock. That person is to watch for news that affects the company, to study research done by Wall Street analysts about the company and to alert the club when it's time to sell.

One person, one stock, makes the challenge of monitoring much easier, but supervising each of your investments is not as daunting a task as it might seem. Remember, you bought the security for a reason. As you review your positions, make sure the reason is still valid. Check with the company periodically by calling its shareholder relations department. The better you know the company, the more pertinent your questions will be. Ask for copies of recent brokerage firm research reports that may have been written about the company. Keep in mind that you won't be sent any unfavorable ones, and only if you really know what questions to ask will you pick up signs of trouble from the company spokesperson. After all, the people who work in a company's shareholder relations department aren't being paid to be negative about the company, although they do have an obligation to be truthful.

Ask your broker to send copies of any pertinent news stories about the company. Brokers can call up several months of news on their quote terminals, and it's very simple to send that information to you.

INVEST OVER TIME

When you find an attractive investment opportunity there is nothing wrong with *averaging into it,* that is, to buy less than a full position initially, with the intent of adding to it. And remember, every day you own a security is a silent, unconscious decision to buy it again. Buying more over time puts that decision to the litmus test. If you aren't really willing to add to your holding, perhaps you shouldn't own it at all. This "buy over time" strategy may help you identify mistakes before they become sizable ones. It will force you to decide never to stop trying to increase your understanding of your investment. Your goal should be to minimize the surprises that can hurt you. The buy over time strategy also illustrates the point that there is no one perfect time to buy or, for that matter, to sell a security. If you wait until you are 100 percent certain, you probably will be too late. Intelligent investing is often the conscious effort and energy involved in trying not to do something stupid.

THE PRICE CAN OFTEN TELL YOU SOMETHING

Pay special attention to significant movement in the company's stock. A sudden spike up or down in its price, accompanied by heavy volume, is worth understanding. Often it is a result of information that isn't public but, by some magic, finds its way into the stock's price. Such a price movement may be a reason to accumulate more or to sell.

Watch out for price movements that seem to defy gravity or are running counter to the overall market. Prices always reflect what someone else is willing to pay, and, more often than not, the price is right.

WHEN TO SELL

Always the most difficult decision an investor faces is the one to *sell*. And yet, every security should be sold at some point. The trick is to identify the point. Because most people miss the precise point, you should come to grips with the realization that, if you made the decision for the right reasons, you made a correct choice. A proper sell discipline is more important than being precisely right with timing.

Most brokers are equally reluctant to recommend a sale, because of all the mistakes that brokers make that clients remember most, selling too early is the worst. People cannot seem to forget selling a stock at $30 that eventually trades at $35, or God forbid, $60. It doesn't matter that the stock was purchased at $10 and the investor tripled his money. Some people actually check the quotes of the stocks they've sold for years, even decades afterward, reminding their broker about every uptick. Getting out of a stock early that might turn into the next Microsoft is a mortal sin in the minds of most clients. (When this sentence was first written, my example was IBM instead of Microsoft. Perhaps that says it all.) So don't depend exclusively on your broker for sell suggestions. Selling can be a gut-wrenching experience. Selling has been compared to getting a divorce. But it really isn't! On Wall Street, a sale should be considered a separation rather than a divorce. Unlike marriage, you can move in and out of relationships with your stocks and convertible bonds, and sometimes you should. It is amazing how objective you can be about a stock or bond you don't own.

There are lots of reasons why people make bad sell decisions. Two of the most popular are:

1. I'm too far ahead.
2. I'm too far behind.

"I'm too far ahead" means the tax incurred by taking the profit would be too great. Is that really true? Let's look at the numbers.

Say you bought 1,000 shares of a stock at $10 a share for a total of $10,000, and now your position is worth $40,000. Under current tax laws, if you sold the stock you would pay Uncle Sam roughly a third of your profits or, in this example, $10,000 ($40,000 current value − $10,000 purchase price = $30,000 profit × 33% tax = $10,000 tax). So you reason the stock would need to fall from $40 to $30, or ten points, simply to justify the tax cost of the sale. You say that's too great a price, so you don't sell.

Now wait a minute! Let's say your reason for wanting to sell turned out to be a valid one and the stock's price falls. Or let's say that the stock's price simply stalls. It doesn't go down, but it doesn't go up either. By not selling, you are writing off the growth potential of the money tied up in that stock. Rather than reinvesting your $30,000 (net after taxes) in a more promising situation, you have tied up $40,000 in an unpromising one. That doesn't make much sense, does it? Don't be blinded by taxes. Try to look at your tax bill not as an indication that you have foolishly enriched the IRS, but as a reminder of just how smart you were for making the investment.

One of the worst investment techniques is to have an investment gear permanently stuck in neutral. Victims of this malady won't sell if the investment goes up, reasoning that it might go up a bit higher. Or, if it goes down, they won't sell because they couldn't take the loss. Practitioners of decisionless investing have elevated their art to a religious state. As a result, their portfolios are usually sad enough to make you cry.

Many people use excuses such as: "I'm too far behind; I can't afford the loss" or "As soon as I get even, I'll get out." Silly people! Why can't they understand that the loss exists whether they choose to take it or not? Waiting to break even may take the rest of their lives. People should forget what they paid for the investment. It is a useless consideration. The real issue is whether your money has the best chance of growing where it is. If not, there are plenty of better places to invest money than in losers. Always view your weakest position as a source of cash for your next investment.

So just when do you sell? You should certainly sell when the reason you made the investment is no longer valid. Every investment should be reviewed continually with this consideration in mind. Say you bought a stock because you suspected the company would be bought or merged. But that didn't happen, and the information you now have suggests that it is less likely to happen. Don't rationalize your decision. Don't invent a new reason to hold. When the bet changes, SELL! Perhaps you bought a stock because you expected a pending order for new business to benefit the company's earnings materially. The order doesn't come through. SELL! Maybe you bought the stock because the analyst thought it had the potential to reach the low $40s. It reaches the low $40s, and the analyst hasn't raised his or her sights. SELL! Maybe you bought a stock for the wrong reason. You made a mistake. Don't get stubborn. Own every investment for a good reason. Don't let your ego say "good buy" when you should be saying "good bye."

Investing is a business of making judgment calls. After you have made them, you can't sit around moaning or second-guessing yourself. You make the best decision you can in the time you have to make it, which is always precious little, and live with the consequences, regardless. That is the way investing will always be. And you will make mistakes. That is inevitable.

The goal is to sell when the downside risk of holding on to the investment outweighs the potential for gain. Don't moan about the possibility of someone else making the last dollar. SELL!

An automatic reason to sell is when there is something better to do with the money. You should always look at your holdings with a view of weaning the weakest and adding to the strongest. Most investors do just the opposite. They sell winners to take profits. After all, it has been said, "You never go broke taking a profit." Bernard

Baruch may have said that but he also died owning shares of a company he had held for a lifetime. It was the reason he died one of the wealthiest men in America of his time. Another simple test: Ask yourself if you would buy more at this price. Or how about, if you didn't own it, would you buy it? If you aren't willing to buy more, chances are others feel the same way. SELL.

Sometimes the reasons to sell are not crystal-clear. Maybe you have a hunch, or you are not entirely convinced that you are making the right decision. Selling in pieces often makes sense. Sell some now. If you turn out to be right and it continues to fall, sell more. If it turns out to be wrong and the stock again begins to climb, you may want to buy more and be happy in the knowledge that you didn't abandon the company entirely for the wrong reason. Or, if you choose not to buy more, at least you will be satisfied that you still own some.

Sometimes companies get sick. Management changes. Management makes mistakes. The environment changes. Just because a company had a blue-chip past doesn't mean it will enjoy an equally rosy future. When the company's earnings start to falter, when cracks begin to appear that make it look less attractive than it once did, do yourself a favor. SELL. You might have to rationalize about your spouse's bulging waistline, his or her graying hair or wrinkles, but you don't owe that to a silly security. Divorce, Wall Street style: SELL.

WHAT ROLE SHOULD YOUR BROKER PLAY?

Using a knowledgeable stockbroker can be a significant advantage. First, he or she is a professional with whom you can discuss ideas concerning strategies and basic buy/sell/hold decisions. Second, he or she is a source of new ideas. Since he or she specializes in investments, you should expect your broker to be a constant source of fresh ideas and to teach you about new investment alternatives. Remember all of the derivative products covered in this book. As new investments emerge, you should learn about them. You may choose not to use any of them but you should at least know they exist and how they work so that you can make an informed choice.

You must have confidence in your broker's honesty, objectivity and judgment. Of course, not all of his or her suggestions will be winners. Brokers are going to make mistakes. From your standpoint, you must be confident that the advice is well-thought-out and that the broker sincerely has your best interest in mind all of the time.

There is a well-understood potential conflict of interest because your broker makes money only when you buy and sell. Keep in mind that long-term relationships exist only when they serve both parties well. You should expect no less than the most carefully considered advice, unmotivated by a sales commission or lack of one. If you feel you are not getting that kind of help, you should look for another broker.

Not all stockbrokers are knowledgeable about convertible securities. It is now easy for you to test your broker's knowledge because you are familiar with such important convertible concepts as conversion premium, conversion ratio, and breakeven period. If it becomes apparent that your broker is unfamiliar with the convertibles, ask to be referred to someone who is. Don't put yourself at the disadvantage of trying to work in this complex field with someone who knows too little, perhaps less than you do.

Expect a broker familiar with convertibles to tell you when a company in which you want to invest offers a convertible. Expect your broker to help you evaluate the convertible and help you make a judgment about whether it offers some advantage over the common stock or straight bond and why. A good broker will at least make you aware of your options. A good broker should also tell you when an attractive convertible is available from a company similar to the one in which you want to invest. Its advantages might cause you to select the convertible in the alternate company over the common stock or straight bond of the company in which you were originally interested.

A knowledgeable broker will help you make decisions about switching from the convertible to the common or straight bond and selling. That kind of advice can add value. It is why you need to work with a broker who has more than a sketchy understanding of convertible securities if convertibles are going to be part of your investment mix.

DOES THE INDIVIDUAL INVESTOR HAVE A CHANCE?

A frequently expressed complaint of individual investors is that they don't stand a chance competing against the high-powered institutions. That is nonsense! Individual investors can be far more versatile, nimble and attuned. Most of us know far more about what is happening in our communities than some New York City based Wall Street analyst. Local knowledge, industry knowledge, people knowledge and product knowledge all can translate into excellent investment ideas. Don't ignore them! And don't ignore your instincts. As an investor, you should always be happy when someone else disagrees with you. Those are the people you will be able to buy from cheaply or sell to dearly.

The more you read, the more likely you are to uncover good ideas worth checking further. Subscriptions to *Forbes, Fortune, Business Week, Money, Kiplinger's Personal Finance Magazine, Smart Money, Changing Times, The Wall Street Journal, Investor's Business Daily, USA Today* and the business section of your local paper are essential. Ideas can also come from investment newsletters. Most superior investors are voracious readers, not only of the financial press but of newspapers and trade magazines. They are constantly looking for ideas and trends. If you don't find at least one investment idea in each of these newspapers and magazines that reimburses you the price of the subscription several times over, you aren't really trying.

Good ideas should also come from your stockbroker. Most brokerage firms pay lots of money to investment analysts whose jobs are to uncover investment ideas for their firm's clients. Your broker has access to those ideas. Assuming he or she knows that you have an interest in those ideas, you should enjoy the same access. A good stockbroker is a source of ideas because he or she is forever on the lookout for good investments. Much of his or her time is spent reading, listening to money managers with ideas, listening to clients' ideas and then sorting out those that make the most sense. There is nothing a good broker wants more than to give you ideas that will make money for you. When that happens you are happy, you will invest even more money and you will refer others who will do the same.

WHERE TO FIND MORE INFORMATION

The Best Kept Secret on Wall Street would be the equivalent to *Convertible Investing 101* if it were taught as a college course. To acquire further knowledge, these books will be of significant value:

Calamos, John P. *Investing in Convertible Securities.* Dearborn Financial Publishing, Inc., 1988.

Fried, Sidney. *Investment and Speculation with Warrants—Options and Convertibles.* R.H.M. Press, 1989.

Noddings, Thomas C. *Convertible Bonds, The Low-Risk, High Profit Alternative To Buying Stocks.* Probus Publishing, 1991.

Pritchard, Jeffrey J. *Investing with Convertible Bonds.* Ballinger Publishing Co., 1990.

Zubulake, Laura A. *The Complete Guide to Convertible Securities Worldwide.* John Wiley & Sons, Inc., 1991.

CHAPTER 10

Convertible Mutual Funds

Mutual funds are professionally managed pools of money. There are thousands of funds. Each has a specific investment objective. Among the thousands of mutual funds are 21 whose objective is to invest in convertible securities. If you are intrigued by the idea of investing part of your money in convertibles, yet would rather have a professional do it for you, consider a convertible mutual fund.

Mutual funds are a good choice for a variety of reasons. It may be that you lack the time or interest that successful investing requires. You are likely not to be very good at managing a convertible securities portfolio unless you are willing to commit the time it takes. Effective convertible management requires you to pay attention to even more factors than you would with a stock and bond portfolio.

Mutual funds also offer a higher level of diversification than most individual investors can achieve on their own. A typical mutual fund portfolio consists of millions of dollars of convertible securities. And these portfolios are managed by some very astute professional investors. It may be that you simply want to take advantage of their expertise and experience. Indeed, if you have read some of the books about convertible securities management, you might have come to the conclusion that the task is too difficult for anyone but a full-time professional. What with strategies such as logarithmic regression, the Black-Scholes Option Model and the Calamos Fair Price Model formula, you may have decided to leave the job to the professionals.

The purpose of this book is to dispel that fear. The book purposefully avoids overly complicated investment techniques that are of little value to most individual investors. However, to take advantage of the talent of professionals who employ those sophisticated investment methods, this is what you need to know about the convertible mutual funds that those experts manage.

MUTUAL FUND TYPES

Mutual funds are either closed-end or open-end. (See Figure 10.1.) *Open-ended mutual funds* issue more shares when you buy into the fund and cancel shares when you sell. Let's assume that you invest $10,000 in an open-end mutual fund. The effect of your investment is that the fund manager has $10,000 more to invest. When you sell $10,000 of an open-end fund the manager has $10,000 less to invest and must reduce his or her total investment portfolio by $10,000 to be able to return money to you.

Closed-end mutual fund shares trade like other common stocks usually on the New York or American Stock Exchanges. Closed-end funds have a fixed number of shares established at the time the fund is created and sold to investors. If you should decide to buy $10,000 of a closed-end fund (other than at the time it is initially offered to the public), you would buy those shares from an investor who is willing to sell. The amount of money the fund manager has to invest would be unaffected as a result of your decision. That amount was raised at the time the shares were originally sold to investors and is more or less than that amount now as a result of the portfolio manager's investment performance.

Open-end fund shares can be more volatile than closed-end shares because if, for some reason, lots of people decide to sell at the same time, the fund manager may have to sell into a weak market to raise money to meet liquidation requests. For example, in 1993, stocks of most health companies tumbled, causing many health care mutual fund investors to decide to redeem their shares. To meet liquidation

FIGURE 10.1 Assets Under Management by Convertible Funds (Open-end and Closed-end)

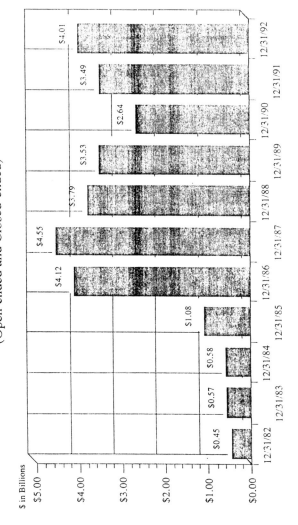

Assets Under Mgt. by Convertible Funds

(Open-ended and Closed-ended)

Source: Reprinted by permission of Smith Barney.

requests, the managers of those funds had to sell shares of the health care companies they owned. Some of the stocks were, no doubt, those the manager would have preferred to hold and perhaps even buy. However, those portfolio managers had no choice but to sell in order to raise the cash they needed to meet the liquidation requests. Obviously, the effect of selling health care stocks into a market that was already weak compounded the losses.

Closed-end fund managers didn't face the same problem. An investor who chose to unload his or her closed-end fund shares sold those shares to another investor on the exchange on which those shares were listed. The fund manager would not have been affected by the investor's decision to sell because the fund manager wouldn't need to sell anything to meet liquidation requests. The liquidation would have occurred on the exchange just as if an investor had decided to sell shares of McDonald's, Merck, Sears or any other common stock.

Price Differences Between Open-End and Closed-End Fund Shares

The price of an open-end mutual fund share is its *net asset value (NAV)*. Net asset value is the total value of the fund portfolio, divided by the number of shares owned by the fund's investors. For example, if the total value of a mutual fund's portfolio on a given day is $100 million and there were 1 million shares outstanding, the NAV would be $10 a share ($100 million ÷ 1 million shares = $10 NAV).

The price of a closed-end mutual fund share is determined by the demand or lack of demand for those shares. That price may be more or less than the net asset value depending on the market for those shares. When the shares trade for more than their NAV, they are trading at a premium. When they trade below their NAV they are trading at a discount to net asset value. Clearly, it is a better deal to buy closed-end fund shares at a discount and avoid paying a premium. You should always want to know what the premium or discount to NAV is in relation to the market price.

Loads and No-Loads

A *load* is a sales fee. Funds that charge no sales fee are called *no-load funds*. Those that charge a sales fee are called *load funds*. There are also funds that charge no-loads when you purchase them but levy a fee when you sell them. They are called *back-end load funds*. Generally, that fee disappears over time. For instance, there may be a 4 percent "surrender charge," or back-end load, to sell the fund the first year you own it, a 3 percent fee the second year, a 2 percent fee the third year, 1 percent the fourth year and no surrender charge from that time forward. There are also *12b-1 funds* that charge no front-end sales fee but subtract a fee each year for the sales expenses of the fund. You can generally move between funds in the same mutual fund family without paying an additional sales fee; that is, you could sell the convertible fund and move that money into the growth stock fund of the same fund family without paying a fee. This type of transaction, however, is a taxable event under current tax laws. If a gain is involved, it is taxable. If a loss is incurred, the loss is deductible.

If you were invested in a back-end fund and, after two years, you switched into another fund in the same back-end fund family, generally the two years would count toward reducing the back-end surrender charge. Also, most load funds don't charge for the automatic reinvestment of dividends and capital gains distributions.

Open-end fund shares are listed under a separate mutual fund table in the financial section of the newspaper. Closed-end fund shares are listed on the exchanges where they trade. The listing for open-end fund shares has two prices for each mutual fund. One of the prices is the NAV per share. The other price is the NAV plus the maximum load the fund can charge. For no-load and back-end loaded funds, the two prices are the same.

The amount of load per share generally decreases with the size of the purchase. That is, an investor who purchases $1,000 of an open-end fund will pay a higher percentage sales fee than an investor who purchases $100,000 of the same fund.

Mutual fund purchases and sales are effective at the end of the trading day. Let's say the market is beginning to rally and you expect share prices to move higher. Even if you place your order to buy a mutual fund at 9:30 in the morning when the market opens, your trade won't be executed until the end of the day. The price you will pay will reflect the activity of the day. It is the same with a market decline. Should the market tumble, regardless of when you place your order to sell your shares, the NAV will be determined at the end of the market day. The total portfolio value is calculated at that time, and the value of your shares will be based on that value.

MUTUAL FUND FACTS

These are some other facts about mutual funds to keep in mind as you consider using them as part of your investment portfolio.

Last year's performance should not be your only measure. Nearly everyone expects last year's best funds to also be next year's winners. Since most investors project the future based on the past, last year's hot fund is the most obvious investment of choice. That is often a mistake. Last year's performance might have resulted from some event or events that are unlikely to repeat or from an investment style that won't work as well when circumstances change. If an investment style is out of vogue, it will be likely to lag the market. Look for a long-term track record from a fund manager who has been there long enough to be responsible for the record. This information is available and important.

Don't use your mutual fund as a checking account. To avoid tax nightmares, never write checks against your fund or sell it in dribs and drabs. Best of all is to own your mutual fund in an account that keeps track of every purchase by share price and purchase date. This is especially important if you are having the dividends automatically reinvested. Establishing cost basis can be a nightmare for a mutual fund with an automatic dividend reinvestment program unless you have a detailed accounting system to help you keep track.

Beware of December purchases.   Mutual funds typically make a capital gains distribution each year in late December. Capital gains result from successful trades of securities inside the fund during the course of the year. As a result, you could invest $20,000 in a fund on December 9th and receive a capital gains distribution of $3,000 on December 24th. Your mutual fund investment would then be $17,000. You would have received $3,000 of your own money and owe a capital gains tax on the $3,000. Invest after the capital gains distribution has occurred.

Understand yield and why it is reported differently.   It is not unusual to see different annualized yield reports for the same mutual fund. That is because the funds themselves and the various services that rank mutual funds calculate yields in different ways.

Some reporting services, including *Money* magazine, use what they call *12-month average yield.* It reports all of the income per share paid by the fund during the past 12 months divided by the most recent NAV. It is a historical number and is no guarantee of what you should expect in the future.

The *Morningstar Mutual Funds* service reports the yield as money actually paid. A more helpful number, however, is a *NAV total return* figure, which Morningstar also reports. Morningstar calculates total return by taking the change in NAV, reinvesting all income and capital gains distributions during the quarter, then dividing that number by the starting net asset value. In the end, the total return figure is the most important one because it tells the investor whether or not he or she made any money. Yields can be manipulated but total return cannot.

The Securities and Exchange Commission (SEC) has its own method of determining yield. It is the yield that is cited in mutual fund advertisements. The SEC method takes into account the income per share over the preceding 30 days (minus expenses), plus or minus adjustments for gains or losses in the portfolio. That is called *marking the portfolio to the market.* It works this way. Certain convertibles will be trading at premiums to their face value. Others will be trading at a discount to their face value. The SEC method requires that before any income is reported, all the bonds in the portfolio must be carried at face value. So, if the market value of the portfolio is $10,000 less than face value, $10,000 is subtracted from the total amount of income the fund earned to bring the value of the portfolio up to face value. The remaining income is divided into the number of shares outstanding to arrive at the income per share. That figure is divided by the fund's offering price per share and then annualized. The SEC method determines a number that is accurate for only one day of the year and supposes that if nothing changed for the entire year, that yield is the one you would earn.

It is important to understand that the income and capital gains or losses change every day in mutual funds because mutual funds are actively managed portfolios. They are affected by changing interest rates and by the changing values of the securities they hold. This is particularly true of funds that invest in convertible securities.

DOLLAR COST AVERAGING

This is a concept that really does work, and yet too few investors do it. The reason so many investors fail to dollar cost average is that the practice violates the most basic of all investor instincts. It requires that investors continue to add to an investment that is declining in price. That is generally when most people stop investing. Most investors are far more comfortable buying when an investment is rising in price. The concept of dollar cost averaging is simple. Invest a fixed amount at regular intervals. Don't worry whether the market is up or down. Have faith that prices will generally move up over time. And remember that while you are regularly contributing to your investment, that act alone coincidentally allows you to accumulate more of an investment.

According to Figure 10.2, nine reinvestments of $1,000, a total of $9,000, could have grown to $10,800, up 20 percent. Note also that during 40 percent of the time, the market value was less than the total amount invested. That is why most people quit the program at precisely the wrong time. The example illustrates that they would

FIGURE 10.2   Dollar Cost Averaging: How $1,000 Invested
Regularly Might Have Grown, Assuming Share
Price Fluctuations

Investment Period	Share Price	Shares Purchased	Cumulative Market Value
1	$ 8	125	$ 1,000
2	10	100	2,250
3	8	125	2,800
4	5	200	2,750
5	4	250	3,200
6	5	200	5,000
7	8	125	9,000
8	10	100	12,250
9	8	125	10,800

Single Investment Value
$9,000

Cumulative Market Value
$10,800

Source: AIM Family of Funds.

have been smarter to increase their contributions when the price was
lower. Isn't the goal, after all, to try to buy low? During the times
the prices are low, you are purchasing more shares at a lower price.
When the price rises, you will own more shares.

CHOOSING A FUND ISN'T YOUR LAST DECISION

You may decide to hire a professional money manager to make
everyday money management decisions for you, but it is still your
money and your responsibility. Monitor your mutual fund's performance just as you would that of an individual stock or bond.
Compare its performance to the performance of the other convertible
funds. If it's lagging the group, figure out why. Compare the perfor-

mance also to the relative market indices such as the Standard & Poor's Index and the Dow Jones Industrial Index.

It is important to give your fund enough time to perform but it is also important to monitor performance and take action when the performance is substandard. Too many investors treat a mutual fund investment as an eternal decision. It's not. A fair measurement period is a full market cycle, which usually extends over a three-year to five-year time horizon. (See Figure 10.3.)

Monitor the performance quarterly, and forget timing services. These are outfits that advise investors when to get in and out of the market. No one can call market turns—absolutely no one! By trading your funds based on perceived blips in the market, you will almost always overmanage your account and contribute to its poor performance.

FIGURE 10.3 Yearly Objective Averages for Three Objectives

Source: Morningstar, Inc.

A CONVERTIBLE FUNDS DIRECTORY

The following is summary information on each of the mutual funds that invest principally in convertible securities. It will give you an idea about how each invests, some performance data and how to contact a fund for a current prospectus. The data for each fund were provided by the fund itself, and though we believe it to be reliable, we cannot guarantee its accuracy.

Name of fund:	**AIM Convertible Securities**
Address:	11 Greenway Plaza
	Suite 1919
	Houston, TX 77046-1173
Phone number:	800-347-1919
Ticker symbol:	CONVX

Investment philosophy:

Fund objective:

Total assets:	$17.2 million as of June 28, 1993
% common stocks:	21.92
% convertible bonds:	58.42
% convertible preferreds:	18.91
% cash:	0
% convertible stocks:	0
% bonds:	0
% government securities:	0
% other:	0

Year fund established:	1978
Fund manager name and start date:	Jonathan Schoolar (1989)
	Wendy Sachnowitz (1989)
Initial investment:	$500.00
Subsequent investment:	$ 50.00
IRA initial investment:	$500.00
IRA annual maintenance fee:	$ 10 per year per account
Management fee:	.75%
Total operating expenses:	2.12%
Front-end load:	4.75%
Deferred sales charge:	0%
12b-1 fee:	.25%
Telephone switch available?	Yes
Account opening procedure:	

Performance:

1-year ending December 31, 1992:	9.64%
5-year ending December 31, 1992:	13.77%
10-year ending December 31, 1992:	8.67%

Name of fund: **Bancroft Convertible Fund, Inc.**
Address: 56 Pine Street
    Suite 1310
    New York, NY 10005
Phone number: 212-269-9236
Ticker symbol: BCV

Investment philosophy: Purchase and hold for income and long-term capital appreciation convertible bonds and preferred stocks. We seek out attractive convertible issues with underlying common stocks that have significant earnings growth potential or that otherwise appear undervalued. We also seek to skew the quality of the portfolio toward investment grade.

Fund objective: Income and the potential for capital appreciation.

Total assets: $63.9 million as of March 31, 1993
  % common stocks: 4.4
  % convertible stocks:
  % convertible bonds: 62.0
  % bonds:
  % convertible preferreds: 28.9
  % government securities: 4.6
  % cash: 0
  % other: 0

Year fund established: 1971
Fund manager name and
  start date: Davis/Dinsmore1970
Initial investment: (closed-end)
Subsequent investment: n/a
IRA initial investment: n/a
IRA annual maintenance fee: n/a
Management fee: 0.75% of assets
Total operating expenses: 1.20% of assets
Front-end load: n/a
Deferred sales charge: n/a
12b-1 fee: n/a
Telephone switch available?   n/a
Account opening procedure: n/a

Performance:
  1-year ending December 31, 1992:   16.06%
  5-year ending December 31, 1992:   70.63%
  10-year ending December 31, 1992:   211.64%

Name of fund:	**Calamos Convertible Fund**
Address:	2001 Spring Road
	Suite 750
	Oak Brook, IL 60521
Phone number:	800-323-9943
Ticker symbol:	CCVIX

Investment philosophy: Utilizing convertible securities, which combine the best of the two investment worlds—the steady cash flow of a bond and the capital appreciation potential of a common stock—the Fund seeks to provide above-average total return with less risk than an investment in a combination of stocks and bonds.

Fund objective: Calamos Convertible Fund seeks current income. Growth is a secondary objective that the Fund also considers when consistent with its objective of current income.

Total assets:	$17,235,746 as of December 31, 1992
% common stocks:	15.48
% convertible stocks:	
% convertible bonds:	59.35
% bonds:	
% convertible preferreds:	19.35
% government securities:	
% cash:	2.5
% other:	3.12

Year fund established:	1985
Fund manager name and start date:	John P. Calamos (September 4, 1990)
Initial investment:	$2,500
Subsequent investment:	$ 100
IRA initial investment:	No minimum
IRA annual maintenance fee:	$ 10
Management fee:	.75%
Total operating expenses:	1.7%
Front-end load:	4.50%
Deferred sales charge:	None
12b-1 fee:	0.50%
Telephone switch available?	No
Account opening procedure:	Complete application

Performance:

1-year ending December 31, 1992:	7.6%
5-year ending December 31, 1992:	11.8%
10-year ending December 31, 1992:	n/a

Name of fund:	**Calamos Strategic Income Fund**
Address:	2001 Spring Road
	Suite 750
	Oak Brook, IL 60521
Phone number:	800-323-9943
Ticker symbol:	CVSIX

Investment philosophy: The Fund uses a unique institutional strategy whereby convertible securities are hedged by the shorting of common stock against the long convertible position. This strategy reduces the portfolio's volatility while increasing current income, providing a combination of secure steady income, growth potential and a stable net asset value.

Fund objective: Strategic Income Fund seeks high current income consistent with stability of principal, primarily through investment in convertible securities and employing short selling to enhance income and hedge against market risk.

Total assets:	$2,204,766 as of December 31, 1992
% common stocks:	(27.80%)
% convertible stocks:	
% convertible bonds:	75.96%
% bonds:	
% convertible preferreds:	19.98%
% government securities:	
% cash:	31.70%
% other:	0.16%

Year fund established:	1990
Fund manager name and start date:	John P. Calamos (September 4, 1990)
Initial investment:	$2,500
Subsequent investment:	$ 100
IRA initial investment:	No minimum
IRA annual maintenance fee:	$ 10
Management fee:	0.75%
Total operating expenses:	2.0%
Front-end load:	Maximum—4.5%
Deferred sales charge:	None
12b-1 fee:	0.50%
Telephone switch available?	No
Account opening procedure:	Complete application

Performance:
1-year ending December 31, 1992:	11.9%
5-year ending December 31, 1992:	n/a
10-year ending December 31, 1992:	n/a

Name of fund: **Calamos Small/Mid Cap Convertible Fund**
Address: 2001 Spring Road
Suite 750
Oak Brook, IL 60521
Phone number: 800-323-9943
Ticker symbol: CVTRX

Investment philosophy: The Fund selects convertible issues of smaller and midsize companies with an emphasis on company fundamentals, accelerating earnings, price growth and financial stability. Special attention is given to companies that are undervalued and poised for future growth.

Fund objective: Calamos Small/Mid Cap Convertible Fund seeks high long-term total return through capital appreciation and current income derived from a diversified portfolio of convertible, equity and fixed-income securities.

Total assets:	$3,091,548 as of December 31, 1992
% common stocks:	5.39
% convertible stocks:	
% convertible bonds:	58.56
% bonds:	
% convertible preferreds:	18.70
% government securities:	
% cash:	12.78
% other:	4.57

Year fund established:	1988
Fund manager name and start date:	John P. Calamos (September 22, 1988)
Initial investment:	$2,500
Subsequent investment:	$ 100
IRA initial investment:	No Minimum
IRA annual maintenance fee:	$ 10
Management fee:	0.75%
Total operating expenses:	2.0%
Front-end load:	Maximum—4.50%
Deferred sales charge:	None
12b-1 fee:	0.50%
Telephone switch available?	No
Account opening procedure:	Complete application

Performance:
1-year ending December 31, 1992: 10.1%
5-year ending December 31, 1992: n/a
10-year ending December 31, 1992: n/a

Name of fund:	**Castle Convertible Fund, Inc.**
Address:	75 Maiden Lane
	New York, NY 10038
Phone number:	800-992-3863
Ticker symbol:	CVF

Investment philosophy: We invest the Fund as a fixed-income vehicle. We use the convertible feature as a means to increase the total return above the returns in the straight debt market.

Fund objective: Current income and possible capital appreciation

Total assets:	$58.1 million as of March 31, 1993
% common stocks:	12.6
% convertible stocks:	0
% convertible bonds:	59.4
% bonds:	0
% convertible preferreds:	21.2
% government securities:	0
% cash:	4.9
% other:	(2.7)

Year fund established:	1971
Fund manager name and start date:	David Alger (1974)
Initial investment:	n/a closed end fund
Subsequent investment:	n/a
IRA initial investment:	n/a
IRA annual maintenance fee:	n/a
Management fee:	.75%
Total operating expenses:	1.06%
Front-end load:	n/a closed end
Deferred sales charge:	n/a
12b-1 fee:	n/a
Telephone switch available?	No
Account opening procedure:	Castle is traded on the American Stock Exchange and may be purchased through one's stock broker.

Performance: (based on NAV)

1-year ending December 31, 1992:	16.1%
5-year ending December 31, 1992:	12.1%
10-year ending December 31, 1992:	10.9%

Name of fund: **Dreyfus Convertible Securities Fund, Inc.**
Address: 200 Park Avenue
                   New York, NY 10166
Phone number: 800-645-6561
Nasdaq symbol: DRCSX

Investment philosophy: Invest primarily in convertible securities and/or synthetic convertibles; the balance of the net assets may be invested in preferred stocks, dividend and nondividend-paying common stocks, U.S. Government securities, corporate bonds, high-grade commercial paper, bankers' acceptance and other short-term instruments

Fund objective: High current income/Capital appreciation

Total assets: $218,951,000 as of December 31, 1992
  % common stocks: 26.12
  % convertible stocks:
  % convertible bonds: 50.27
  % bonds: 0.47
  % convertible preferreds: 25.22
  % government securities: n/a
  % cash: (2.08)
  % other: n/a

Year fund established: 1971
Fund manager name and
  start date: Catherine Jacobson (1990)
Initial investment: $2,500
Subsequent investment: $ 100
IRA initial investment: $ 750
IRA annual maintenance fee: $ 10
Management fee: 0.75%
Total operating expenses: 1.01%
Front-end load: None
Deferred sales charge: None
12b-1 fee: None
Telephone switch available?   Yes
Account opening procedure: Check plus application

Performance:
  1-year ending March 31, 1993:   4.70%
  5-year ending March 31, 1993:   8.66%
  10-year ending March 31, 1993:   11.75%

Name of fund: **Ellsworth Convertible Growth and Income Fund, Inc.**

Address: 56 Pine Street
                 Suite 1310
                 New York, NY 10005
Phone number: 212-269-9236
Ticker symbol: ECF

Investment philosophy: Purchase and hold convertible securities for long term growth and income. We seek convertible bonds and preferred stocks that appear attractive to us. Further, the underlying common stocks must have a potential for growth based on value, earnings potential or economy/industry growth. We seek to skew the average quality of the portfolio towards investment grade.

Fund objective: Growth and Income using convertible securities augmented by covered call writing and economic hedging.

Total assets: $61.9 million as of June 28, 1993
  % common stocks: 4.5
  % convertible stocks: 0
  % convertible bonds: 63.5
  % bonds: 0
  % convertible preferreds: 30.0
  % government securities: 2.4
  % cash: 0.1
  % other: 0

Year fund established: 1986
Fund manager name and
  start date: Davis/Dinsmore (1970)
Initial investment: n/a (closed-end)
Subsequent investment: n/a
IRA initial investment: n/a
IRA annual maintenance fee: n/a
Management fee: 0.75% of net assets
Total operating expenses: 1.2% of net assets
Front-end load: n/a
Deferred sales charge: n/a
12b-1 fee: n/a
Telephone switch available?   n/a
Account opening procedure: n/a

Performance:
  1-year ending December 31, 1992:   16.32%
  5-year ending December 31, 1992:   73.77%
  10-year ending December 31, 1992: n/a

Name of fund:	**Fidelity Convertible Securities Fund**
Address:	Fidelity Investments
	82 Devonshire Street
	Boston, MA 02109
Phone number:	800-544-8888
Ticker symbol:	FCVSX.Q

Investment philosophy: Equity-minded; focuses on convertible issues from companies whose growth potential has been demonstrated by above-average earnings.

Fund objective: Seeks a high level of total return through a combination of current income and capital appreciation by investing primarily in convertible securities.

Total assets:	$725,000,000 as of March 31, 1993
% common stocks:	8
% convertible stocks:	0
% convertible bonds:	51
% bonds:	0
% convertible preferreds:	31
% government securities:	0
% cash:	9
% other:	0

Year fund established:	January 5, 1987
Fund manager name and start date:	Andrew Offit (March 1992)
Initial investment:	$2,500
Subsequent investment:	$ 250
IRA initial investment:	$ 500
IRA annual maintenance fee:	For balance < $5000 = $10, balance > $5,000 = $0
Management fee:	.54%
Total operating expenses:	.96%
Front-end load:	0.00%
Deferred sales charge:	0.00%
12b-1 fee:	None
Telephone switch available?	Yes
Account opening procedure:	Mail, phone or in person

Performance:

1-year ending December 31, 1992:	22.02%
5-year ending December 31, 1992:	19.19%
Life of Fund:	14.81%

Name of fund:	**Harbor Fund**
Address:	2800 Post Oak Boulevard
	Houston, Texas
Phone number:	713-993-0500
Ticker symbol:	ACHBX

Investment philosophy: Philosophy is centered around large, well-capitalized companies with growth and income prospects. Security selection up process which concentrates upon the unique characteristics of each company and involves evaluation of management, financial strength, profitability and the proprietary nature of operations, technology and marketing.

Fund objective: Current income, capital appreciation, reasonable protection of capital through investing primarily in quality-oriented convertible bonds.

Total assets:	$440,000,000
% common stocks:	16
% convertible stocks:	0
% convertible bonds:	54
% bonds:	7
% convertible preferreds:	22
% government securities:	0
% cash:	1
% other:	0

Year fund established:	1956
Fund manager name and start date:	James Behrmann (October 1984)
Initial investment:	$500
Subsequent investment:	$ 25
IRA initial investment:	same
IRA annual maintenance fee:	$ 15
Management fee:	0.59% max/ 0.35 min
Total operating expenses:	1%
Front-end load:	5.75%
Deferred sales charge:	None
12b-1 fee:	.18%
Telephone switch available?	Yes
Account opening procedure:	Prospectus application

Performance:

1-year ending December 31, 1992:	9.72%
5-year ending December 31, 1992:	87.81%
10-year ending December 31, 1992:	209.43%

Name of fund: **HT Insight Convertible Fund**
Address: 111 West Monroe
                 Lower Level West
                 Chicago, IL 60603
Phone number: 312-461-6000
Ticker symbol:

Investment philosophy:

Fund objective: The Fund seeks to provide capital appreciation and current income by investing, under normal circumstances, at least 65% of its assets in securities such as bonds, debentures, notes, preferred stocks or warrants convertible into common stock.

Total assets:	$8,000,000
% common stocks:	
% convertible stocks:	18
% convertible bonds:	69
% bonds:	
% convertible preferreds:	
% government securities:	5
% cash:	8
% other:	

Year fund established:	1988
Fund manager name and start date:	Thomas Corkill (November 1, 1992)
Initial investment:	$1,000
Subsequent investment:	$ 250
IRA initial investment:	$1,000
IRA annual maintenance fee:	$ 50
Management fee:	25 basis points
Total operating expenses:	80 basis points
Front-end load:	4.5%
Deferred sales charge:	None
12b-1 fee:	None
Telephone switch available?	Yes
Account opening procedure:	Contact Harris Investors Direct, Inc. 312-461-6000

Performance:
    1-year ending December 31, 1992:   15.40%
    5-year ending December 31, 1992:   7.56%
    10-year ending December 31, 1992: n/a

Name of fund:	**Institutional Investors Convertible Securities Fund, Inc.**
Address:	330 Madison Avenue 8th Floor New York, NY 10017
Phone number:	212-551-1920
Ticker symbol:	n/a

Investment philosophy: The fund seeks to achieve its objectives by investing primarily in a diversified portfolio of fixed income securities convertible into common stock, such as convertible corporate notes, bonds, and debentures, convertible preferred stocks and "synthetic" convertible units consisting of nonconvertible debt securities coupled with detachable warrants.

Fund objective: Primary objective: To obtain current income through investing principally in fixed income securities convertible into common stock. Secondary Objective: Capital appreciation

Total assets:	$2,691,307
% common stocks:	
% convertible stocks:	
% convertible bonds:	68.7
% bonds:	
% convertible preferreds:	21.0
% government securities:	
% cash:	10.3
% other:	

Year fund established:	July 15, 1985
Fund manager name and start date:	Mark F. Troutman (March 9, 1993)
Initial investment:	$20,000.00
Subsequent investment:	Not set
IRA initial investment:	n/a
IRA annual maintenance fee:	n/a
Management fee:	.75% of first 1% of the first $75,000,000 average daily net assets
Total operating expenses:	December 31, 1992 ratio of expenses to average net assets 2.56%
Front-end load:	None
Deferred sales charge:	None
12b-1 fee:	0
Telephone switch available?	n/a
Account opening procedure:	Open to eligible savings institutions

Performance:

1-year ending December 31, 1992:	15.3%
5-year ending December 31, 1992:	8.2%
Since August, 1985:	6.5%

Name of fund: **Lexington Convertible Securities Fund**
Address: P.O. Box 1515
                 Park 80 West Plaza Two
                 Saddle Brook, NJ 07662
Phone number: 800-526-0056
Ticker symbol: CNCVX

Investment philosophy: Our Fund's investment philosophy focuses on total
   return, which we seek to achieve by providing capital appreciation and
   current income while emphasizing preservation of capital. We seek to
   accomplish this through the use of convertible securities that can be exchanged into the common stock of companies or emerging earnings growth.

Fund objective: Capital appreciation, current income and conservation of
   capital

Total return: 1-year—13.2; 5-year—11.25; year-to-date—4.22

Total assets:	$7 million as of June 28, 1993
% common stocks:	44.2
% convertible stocks:	
% convertible bonds:	49.5
% bonds:	
% convertible preferreds:	0.0
% government securities:	
% cash:	6.3
% other:	

Year fund established*:	1988
Fund manager name and start date:	Richard B. Russell (February 1988)
Initial investment:	$1,000
Subsequent investment:	$ 50
IRA initial investment:	$1,000
IRA annual maintenance fee:	$12/customer
Management fee:	1.00%
Total operating expenses**:	2.32%
Front-end load:	None
Deferred sales charge:	None
12b-1 fee:	0.25%
Telephone switch available?	Yes
Account opening procedure:	Call Lexington Representative at (800) 526-0056

Performance:
   1-year ending December 31, 1992:   12.82%
   5-year ending December 31, 1992:   n/a
   10-year ending December 31, 1992:   n/a

*Fund was formerly Concord Income Trust: Convertible Portfolio
**Net of reimbursement/waiver

Name of fund:	**Liberty-Equity Income Fund**
Address:	Federated Investors
	Federated Investors Tower
	1001 Liberty Avenue
	Pittsburgh, PA 15222
Phone number:	412-288-6641
Ticker symbol:	LEIFX

Investment philosophy: Invests mostly in utilities. Lowest-risk utility fund possible.

Fund objective: Above average current income capital appreciation.

Total assets:
% common stocks:	63.48
% convertible stocks:	0
% convertible bonds:	0
% bonds:	3.24
% convertible preferreds:	0
% government securities:	0
% cash:	7.29
% other:	25.99

Year fund established:	1986
Fund manager name and start date:	Chris Wiles (1990)
Initial investment:	$500
Subsequent investment:	$100
IRA initial investment:	$ 50
IRA annual maintenance fee:	No IRA fee
Management fee:	
Total operating expenses:	1.05
Front-end load:	4.05
Deferred sales charge:	0.00
12b-1 fee:	0.25
Telephone switch available?	Yes
Account opening procedure:	Direct through a broker/dealer

Performance:
1-year ending December 31, 1992:	9.80%
5-year ending December 31, 1992:	15.06%
10-year ending December 31, 1992:	n/a

Name of fund: **Lincoln National Convertible Securities Fund**
Address: 1300 South Clinton St.
   Fort Wayne, IN 46801
Phone number: 219-455-2210
Ticker symbol: LNV

Investment philosophy: To look more at growth with convertibles by holding them out or converting into different issues—all with a gain.

Fund objective: Provides a high level of total return through a combination of capital appreciation and current income.

Total assets: $117,778,000 as of March 31, 1993
   % common stocks: 1
   % convertible stocks: 0
   % convertible bonds: 42
   % bonds: 0
   % convertible preferreds: 55
   % government securities: 0
   % cash: 2
   % other: 0

Year fund established: 1986
Fund manager name and
   start date: Lynch & Mayer, Inc.
Initial investment: n/a
Subsequent investment: n/a
IRA initial investment: n/a
IRA annual maintenance fee: n/a
Management fee: .6% Inc Administration
Total operating expenses: 0.83%
Front-end load:
Deferred sales charge:
12b-1 fee:
Telephone switch available?
Account opening procedure:

Performance:
   1-year ending December 31, 1992:   11.7
   5-year ending December 31, 1992:   17.3
   10-year ending December 31, 1992:   n/a

Name of fund: **Nicholas-Applegate Income & Growth Fund**
Address: P.O. Box 8237
                Boston, MA 02266
Phone number: 800-551-8043
Ticker symbol: NAIGX A
                NIGBX B

Investment philosophy:
1. Bottom-up: individual security selection
2. Fully invested
3. Buys securities of companies demonstrating:
   A. Earnings acceleration
   B. Sustainability of earnings growth
   C. Positive relative price strength

Fund objective: To invest in small to midcap comanies with a portfolio structure that provides attractive current income, downside protection and participation with the common stocks on the upside.

Total assets: $15 million as of May 11, 1993
  % common stocks: 30-35
  % convertible stocks: 0
  % convertible bonds: 40-50
  % bonds: 0
  % convertible preferreds: 30-15
  % government securities: 0
  % cash: 0-5
  % other: 0

Year fund established: 1993 (The fund is a conversion from a
                              previously managed limited partnership.)
Fund manager name and   John D. Wylie (May 1987)
  start date:
Initial investment: $2,000
Subsequent investment:
IRA initial investment: $2,000
IRA annual maintenance fee:
Management fee: 75 Basis Points
Total operating expenses: Max of 1.60 bp on A shares;
                              2.25 on B shares

Front-end load: 5.25%
Deferred sales charge: 1%
12b-1 fee:
Telephone switch available? Yes
Account opening procedure: A shares—by telephone with application in
                              prospectus; B shares—through
                              broker/dealer with selling agreement.

Performance:
    1-year ending December 31, 1992:   15.89%
    5-year ending December 31, 1992:   22.23%
    10-year ending December 31, 1992: 21.34%

Name of fund: **Pacific Horizon Capital Income Fund**
Address: Concord Financial Group, Inc.
                   125 West 55th Street
                   11th Floor
                   New York, NY 10019
Phone number: 800-332-3863
Ticker symbol: PACIX

Investment philosophy: Invest in growing companies to seek growth of capital
   and increase income by the use of convertible securities.

Fund objective: The Fund seeks to provide a high total return composed of
   current income and capital appreciation.

Total assets: $19,420,999 as of fund year-end
                                   February 28, 1993
   % common stocks: 13.2
   % convertible stocks: 0
   % convertible bonds: 46.4
   % bonds: 0
   % convertible preferreds: 32.8
   % government securities: .6
   % cash: 7
   % other: 0

Year fund established: 1987
Fund manager name and
   start date: Bill Hensor (August 1987)
Initial investment: $1,000
Subsequent investment: $ 100
IRA initial investment: $ 750
IRA annual maintenance fee: $10 per fund per account
Management fee: 65 BP main & admin fee currently waived
                                   as of February 28, 1993
Total operating expenses: 2.59% of this 2.52% was waived as of
                                   February 28, 1993
Front-end load: 4.50%
Deferred sales charge: n/a
12b-1 fee: 10 BP currently being waived as of
                                   February 28, 1993
Telephone switch available?   Yes
Account opening procedure: By application direct to fund through a
                                   broker/dealer who has a signed selling
                                   group agreement.

Performance:
   1-year ending December 31, 1992:   21.34%
   5-year ending December 31, 1992:   curr 136.65% annualized 18.8%
   10-year ending December 31, 1992: n/a

Name of fund: **Phoenix Convertible Fund**
Address: 100 Bright Meadow Boulevard
                  Enfield, CT 06109
Phone number: 800-243-4361
Ticker symbol: PHCVX

Investment philosophy: The fund employs a consistent long-term philosophy. The Phoenix Fund has a top-down approach to investing. The first step is to analyze the overall economy. From this macro-view, business sectors and industries will be identified that will potentially benefit from upcoming economic conditions. Lastly, individual investments will be chosen with strict guidelines. These are: all companies must be able to show stability and earning momentum and are generally high quality corporations. The fund group also uses a strict sell discipline to protect profits. The Phoenix Convertible fund is the most conservative of all equity oriented funds in the Phoenix Funds family.

Investment Objective: The fund's objectives are both income and capital appreciation which are considered relatively equal.

Total assets: $231.5 million as of June 23, 1993
  % common stocks: 12
  % convertible stocks: 0
  % convertible bonds: 65
  % bonds: 0
  % convertible preferreds: 3
  % government securities: 1
  % cash: 19
  % other: 0

Year fund established: September 1970
Fund manager name and
  start date: John Hamlin (August 1992)
Initial investment: $500
Subsequent investment: $ 25
IRA initial investment: $ 25
IRA annual maintenance fee: $ 10 set up $20 yearly
Management fee: .71%
Total operating expenses: 1.20%
Front-end load: 4.75% less than $50,000
Deferred sales charge: None
12b-1 fee: .25%
Telephone switch available?   Yes
Account opening procedure: Prospectus application and wire order

Performance:

	POP		NAV	
1-year ending January 31, 1992:	POP	7.6%	NAV	12.9%
5-year ending January 31, 1992:		9.7%		10.7%
10-year ending January 31, 1992:		12.8%		13.3%

Name of fund:	**SBSF Convertible Securities Fund**
Address:	45 Rockefeller Plaza
	New York, NY
Phone number:	800-422-SBSF
Ticker symbol:	SBFLX Q

Investment philosophy: The Fund will invest at least 65% of net assets in convertible securities, although it is not required to sell securities in order to maintain this percentage. These will generally be rated from BBB to CCC. The balance of fund assets may be invested in preferred stocks, dividend- and nondividend-paying common stocks, U.S. government securities, corporate bonds and money market instruments of various kinds.

Fund Objective: The Fund's investment objective is to seek a high level of current income together with long-term capital appreciation. The Fund invests primarily in bonds, corporate notes, preferred stocks and other securities convertible into common stocks.

Total assets:	$56,060,707
% common stocks:	18.44
% convertible stocks:	0
% convertible bonds:	26.79
% bonds:	9
% convertible preferreds:	28.87
% government securities:	16.09
% cash:	.81
%other:	0

Year fund established:	1988
Fund manager name and start date:	Louis R. Benzak (April 14, 1988)
Initial investment:	$5,000
Subsequent investment:	$ 100
IRA initial investment:	$ 500
IRA annual maintenance fee:	$ 10
Management fee:	.75%
Total operating expenses:	1.32%
Front-end load:	None
Deferred sales charge:	None
12b-1 fee:	.25%
Telephone switch available?	Yes
Account opening procedure:	

Investors may purchase shares of the fund on any day on which the New York Stock Exchange is open for business. There are no sales commissions.

Purchases may be made by mailing a check payable to SBSF Convertible Securities Fund, c/o Mutual Funds Service Co., P.O. Box 2798, Boston, MA 02208-2798. The check must be accompanied by a completed subscription order form.

Performance:
    1-year ending December 31, 1992:   11.3%
    5-year ending December 31, 1992:   76.2% (from inception April 14,
                                              1988 to December 31, 1992)
    10-year ending December 31, 1992: n/a

Name of fund: **Shearson Lehman Brothers Income**
                  Funds—Convertible Fund
Address: Shearson Lehman Advisors
                  2 World Trade Center
                  New York, NY 10048
Phone number: 212-720-9218
Ticker symbol: SCVSX.Q

Investment philosophy: The Fund strategy is to focus on investment-grade convertible securities with attractive total return opportunities. Special emphasis is placed on convertible securities with "favorable leverage" or convertibles with greater upside equity participation compared to downside risk.

Fund objective: Fund seeks current income and capital appreciation by investing in convertible debentures and convertible preferred stocks. Under normal conditions, fund will invest at least 65% of its assets in convertible securities.

Total assets:	$63,256,472
% common stocks:	
%convertible stocks:	
% convertible bonds:	59
% bonds:	
% convertible preferreds:	35
% government securities:	
% cash:	6
% other:	

Year fund established:	1986
Fund manager name and start date:	Jack Levande/Robert Swab (October 1990)
Initial investment:	$1,000
Subsequent investment:	$ 200
IRA initial investment:	$ 250
IRA annual maintenance fee:	
Management fee:	.70%
Total operating expenses:	1.88%
Front-end load:	5% class A shares
Deferred sales charge:	5% class B shares—declines to 0% after 5 years
12b-1 fee:	.25% class A shares .75% class B shares
Telephone switch available?	No
Account opening procedure:	At Shearson Lehman Bros. Branch offices

Performance:	SEC (annualized)	Lipper (cumulative)	Lipper (annualized)
1-year ending 12/31/92:	8.45%	13.47%	13.47%
5-year ending 12/31/92:	10.15%	63.24%	10.30%
10-year ending 12/31/92:	n/a	n/a	n/a

Name of fund: **TCW Convertible Securities Fund (closed-end)**
Address: TCW Funds Management, Inc.
                 865 S. Figueroa Street
                 Los Angeles, CA 90017
Phone number: 213-244-0000
Ticker symbol: CVT

Investment philosophy: The investment objective of the Fund is to have a total
    return that captures the vast majority of equity returns over a full market
    cycle with lower-than-average volatility. This will be accomplished through
    the use of convertible securities that capture most of the upside during
    bullish periods while declining substantially less than the overall market
    during down markets. The overall volatility of the Fund is expected to be
    meaningfully less than that of the S & P 500.
The Fund has adopted a fundamental policy that under normal market condi-
    tions it will invest at least 65% of its total assets in convertible securities;
    historically, the Fund has always been at least 90% invested in convertible
    securities. The dividend policy of the Fund was changed in mid-1988 to
    reflect the long-term total return expectation of the Fund. The dividend rate
    of $0.21 per quarter has been paid consistently since 1988. Dividends are
    paid from dividend and interest income, realized capital gains, and, if
    necessary, from a return of capital.

Total assets: $215,207,705 as of December 31, 1992
    % common stocks: 1.0
    % convertible stocks: 71.6
    % convertible bonds: 0.0
    %bonds: 0.3
    % convertible preferreds: 24.7
    % government securities:
    % cash: 1.6
    %other: 0.8

Year fund established: March 5, 1987
Fund manager name and
    start date: Howard Marks, Larry Keele, Kevin Hunter
                               (1987)
                           Bob Hanisee (1992)
Initial investment: Listed on NYSE
Subsequent investment: Listed on NYSE
IRA initial investment: n/a
IRA annual maintenance fee: n/a
Management fee: .75% on first 100 million,
                            .50% > $100 million
Total operating expenses: .88% (Ratio of expenses to average
                               net assets)
Front-end load: 0.00%
Deferred sales charge: 0.00%
12b-1 fee: 0.00%
Telephone switch available? n/a
Account opening procedure: n/a

Performance:

    1-year ending December 31, 1992: 14.5%
    5-year ending December 31, 1992: 79.6%
  10-year ending December 31, 1992: n/a

Name of fund:	**The Bond Fund For Growth—Rochester Fund Series***
Address:	70 Linden Oaks
	Rochester, NY 14625
Phone number:	716-383-1300
Ticker symbol:	RCVGX

Investment philosophy: We believe that convertible bonds, an asset class that provides attractive fixed returns in addition to appreciation potential, offer the best opportunity to achieve real rates of return while minimizing risk. As you know, convertible bonds are an investment vehicle that combines some of the most favorable advantages of both straight bonds and common stocks, providing attractive fixed returns in addition to appreciation potential.

At Rochester, we believe that all investment characteristics are relative. We utilize a ranking system that assigns points and relative weightings for fundamental and statistical characteristics. This investment process is designed to promote issues with strong risk/reward profiles.

A review of the enclosed Bond Fund For Growth portfolio will show our investment approach, including our participation in the full breadth of the convertible market from:

- small-cap to large-cap
- service industries to manufacturing
- short maturity to long maturity
- stable industries to cyclical industries
- high financial strength to low financial strength

We categorize our convertible holdings into the following four groupings which are further detailed in the attached letter to financial consultants:

1. Traditional Convertibles
2. Broken Convertibles
3. Short Effective Maturity Convertibles
4. Equity Substitute Convertibles

In our professional opinion, each holding offers a strong risk/reward profile. Thus, we believe that the Fund will generate competitive total returns with less volatility than the market in general over the coming years.

Fund objective: The Fund seeks long-term growth and current income through investment in a portfolio consisting of a variety of convertible fixed income securities, convertible bonds and convertible preferred stocks. The Fund will emphasize investments in convertible securities issued by small-size to medium-size companies.

Total assets:	$23,269,820 as of March 31, 1993
% common stocks:	3.0
% convertible stocks:	
% convertible bonds:	79.5
% bonds:	
% convertible preferreds:	7.7
% government securities:	
% cash:	9.8
% other:	

Year fund established:	1986
Fund manager name and start date:	Michael S. Rosen (Since inception)
Initial investment:	$2,000
Subsequent investment:	$ 100
IRA initial investment:	$2,000
IRA annual maintenance fee:	None for 1993
Management fee:	.47%
Total operating expenses:	1.91%
Front-end load:	3.25%
Deferred sales charge:	n/a
12b-1 fee:	.75%
Telephone switch available?	With form on file
Account opening procedure:	Broker/dealer

Performance:	Annualized		Cumulative	
	NAV	MOP	NAV	MOP
1-year ending 12/31/92:	31.2%	27.0%	88.3%	82.0%
5-year ending 12/31/92:	13.5%	12.7%	88.3%	82.0%
10-year ending 12/31/92:	8.4%	7.9%	70.0%	64.4%

For period ending December 31, 1992 MOP = Maximum Offering Price

*Formerly the Rochester Convertible Fund

Name of fund:	**Thomson Equity Income Fund**
Address:	One Station Place
	Stamford, CT 06902
Phone number:	800-628-1237
Ticker symbol:	TQNAX/TQNBX

Investment philosophy: Positive momentum and positive surprise. This investment strategy suggests that a good company doing better than generally expected will experience a rise in its stock price and therefore signifies a buy opportunity.

Fund objective: Current income and long-term growth of capital

Total assets:
% common stocks:	37.5
% convertible stocks:	
% convertible bonds:	34.2
% bonds:	3.0
% convertible preferreds:	14.6
% government securities:	
% cash:	10.7
% other:	

Year fund established:	A shares (February 4, 1991) B shares
	(April 18, 1988)
Fund manager name and start date:	Amy Hogan (December 1990)
	Irvin Smith (April 1988)
Initial investment:	$1,000
Subsequent investment:	$ 100
IRA initial investment:	$ 25
IRA annual maintenance fee:	
Management fee:	A shares .75% B shares .75%
Total operating expenses:	A shares 1.35% B shares 2.10%
Front-end load:	5.5% max
Deferred sales charge:	1% in 1st year
12b-1 fee:	A shares .25% B shares 1.0%
Telephone switch available?	Yes
Account opening procedure:	Through broker/dealer or call toll free
	number for investor guide with
	prospectus and application

Performance:
1-year ending December 31, 1992:	A shares 8.67% B shares 7.78%
5-year ending December 31, 1992:	n/a
10-year ending December 31, 1992:	n/a

Name of fund: **Value Line Convertible Fund, Inc.**
Address: 711 3rd Ave
                  New York, NY 10017-4064
Phone number: 1-800-223-0818
Ticker symbol: VALCX

Investment philosophy: Value Line Convertible Fund, Inc. (the "Fund") is a no-load diversified, open-end management company whose investment objective is to seek high current income together with capital appreciation. The Fund seeks to accomplish its objective by investing primarily in convertible securities.

Fund objective: High current income, capital appreciation. At least 70% convertible securities.

Total assets: $41,163,000 as of June 28, 1993
  % common stocks:
  % convertible stocks:
  % convertible bonds: 65.2
  % bonds:
  % convertible preferreds: 25.5
  % government securities: 4.3
  % cash & rec.:   1.3
  % other (repo):   3.7

Year fund established: 1985
Fund manager name and
  start date: Value Line, Inc. Team (January 1990)
Initial investment: $1,000
Subsequent investment: $ 250
IRA initial investment: $1,000
IRA annual maintenance fee: $ 10
Management fee: .0075 of average daily net assets
Total operating expenses: 1.20% annualized as of 10/31/92
Front-end load: None
Deferred sales charge: None
12b-1 fee: None
Telephone switch available? Yes
Account opening procedure: By mail

Performance:
  1-year ending December 31, 1992:   13.83%
  5-year ending December 31, 1992:   12.62%
  June 3, 1985–December 31, 1992:   10.87%

CHAPTER 11

Do's and Don'ts: Reminders That May Save You Money

Do

Always check first to see if there is a convertible trading for the same company, when you are buying a common stock.

Don't

Assume that just because it is a convertible that it is a better buy than the common.

Do

Always buy the convertible if it trades at or close to parity (that is, the market price of the convertible is equal or close to equal to the value of the common into which the convertible can be exchanged)—assuming of course, that the convertible pays a greater amount of income.

Don't

Buy the convertible if the conversion premium is high, without considering the risks of a takeover or merger that could turn your convertible into a straight bond.

Do

Try to improve your investment position by using converts to reduce your risk and increase your return by switching out of the common when the premium is small and back into the common when it is high.

Don't

Assume the convert is always the best way to own a stake in a company.

Do

Be patient. Give good ideas a chance to work out. Most investing involves waiting for good things to happen. Lack of patience is the single biggest impediment to success among investors.

Don't

Stay with an investment if the reason you made the investment no longer applies.

Do

Always determine how the convert can be taken away from you. Assume it will if it is to the issuer's advantage.

Don't

Ignore the people running the company. Ethical people with high standards are better bets than those with little of either quality.

Do

Remember excesses always last much longer than anyone thinks possible, but longevity is not a sound reason for believing they are not excesses.

Don't

Forget that excesses always correct themselves.

Do

Know what you own.

Don't

Forget that the Forecasters' Hall of Fame is an empty room. The market is more than unpredictable; it is perverse!

Do

Diversify. A well-rounded portfolio containing various mixes of assets can iron out a lot of ups and downs in investing.

Do

Keep winners. Sell losers. The market is ultimately anchored by fundamentals. Irrational price movements away from those fundamentals will eventually be reversed. You sometimes need the patience of a saint to buy and hold, but then you will be a very rich saint.

Don't

Buy losers instead of winners. Silly advice? How many times do people ignore stocks just because they have already appreciated significantly? "How much higher could it possibly go?" they ask. Forget that. What a stock has done in the past has nothing at all to do with what it will do in the future. It's a better bet that its price will continue to climb than that you will find a loser that turns into a winner.

Do

Be mindful that the market always does what it will to baffle the largest number of participants. Try not to be too shocked when the unexpected happens and the expected doesn't.

Don't

Fight the tape. When prices go up or down with conviction, the market is telling you something and your being stubborn about accepting it isn't going to change anything. To paraphrase a song title, "I Fought the Tape, and the Tape Won."

Do

Check the call provisions of any convertible that you want to buy at a premium. If, for example, the convert is trading at 111, its parity is 106 and its call price is 104½, you stand to lose the difference between 111 and 106 if it is called.

Don't

Let a high yield be your only reason for buying a convert. If the conversion premium is high, evaluate the convert as you would any high-yield security. The conversion feature is an extra that may never come into play. Never underestimate the risk of poor judgment. A buyout, merger, partial liquidation or sale of assets could cause the bond's price to fall even further and the equity kicker won't protect you.

Do

Know that bargain investments are not necessarily those with cheap prices. It's better to buy a good convert at a fair price than a fair convertible at a good price.

Don't

Forget that there are exceptions to every rule and that those exceptions often become the rule.

Do

Know that security prices of good companies come back when the market returns; speculative securities come back only some of the time.

G L O S S A R Y

Terms Applying to the Convertible Market Place

accrued interest Interest earned on a bond since the last interest payment date. The buyer of the bond pays the market price plus accrued interest to the seller and is entitled to the next interest coupon in full. Exceptions include bonds in default and bonds that are traded flat (without accrued interest).

adjustment of conversion terms Changes in conversion terms, which may be provided for under the terms of the conversion privilege or warrant based on the passage of time, the conversion of a certain amount of convertibles or by virtue of the operation of an antidilution clause.

aggressive grade Those below investment grade; in other words, junk.

anti-dilution clause Provisions contained in most convertibles and warrants that may call for the adjustment of the conversion terms in the case of stock dividends, stock splits or the sale of common stock (directly or via issuance of new convertibles) below the conversion price of existing warrants and convertibles. Often no adjustment is required for stock dividends under 2 percent to 5 percent in any year.

arbitrage A simultaneous purchase and sale of identical or similar securities to take advantage of price differences created by the market.

asset-linked convertibles Convertibles linked to precious metals instead of common stock (gold, silver, oil and real estate). An extension of the gold-linked certificates used in the past. *Example:* Sunshine Mines issued a 15-year, 8½ percent corporate convertible into silver at $20 an ounce.

at a discount Below par value (par is 100). A bond is said to be selling at a discount when its market value is below the par value payable at maturity. *Example:* A $1,000 bond selling at $850. It would be quoted as selling at 85% of par, or 85.

at a premium Above par or face value. *Example:* A $1,000 bond selling at $1,150, quoted as 115. A bond will trade above the amount payable at maturity if the yield is higher than normal or if a valuable conversion privilege influences the price of the bond more than the yield alone.

basis value The rate of interest on a bond or obligation that serves as the basis on which bond values are compared and traded. Because the value of a straight senior security is determined by its yield and the going interest rate level, the basis value is obtained from special tables that take into account the annual rate, the going rate and the time to maturity.

bearer bond A bond whose interest and principal are payable to its holder without specifying any name. The opposite of registered bond.

bond A certificate of debt: an IOU issued by a government, municipality or corporation to the lender of money. It represents a binding agreement between the issuer and the bond holder, whereby the issuer promises to pay interest on a regular basis and to repay the face amount on a specified date.

bond indenture The contract instrument under which bonds are issued. It describes such terms of the agreement as rate of interest, date of maturity, redemption terms, conversion privilege and security for the loan.

bond price quotation Bond prices are quoted as a percentage of par. Thus, 98 means 98 percent of a $1,000 bond, or $980 per bond. If a bond trades in $100 denominations, 98 means 98 percent of $100, or $98 per bond. 105½ means 105.5 percent of par.

bottom fishers Investors who try to buy securities of distressed companies at the lowest levels, hoping for an upturn.

breakeven time The time period in which an investment in a convertible bond or convertible preferred stock will recapture the premium over conversion value because of the convertible's higher yield. Breakeven time is usually expressed in years and is calculated on the assumption that the common dividend will remain the same. It is calculated with this formula: amount of the premium over the conversion value in percentage points divided by the yearly extra dividend income in dollars. Also referred to as premium recovery, or payback period.

call An option to buy securities under specified terms that usually include the price, the time period and the number of shares. *See* puts and calls. Also means an option by a corporation to redeem senior securities at a fixed price or other preset terms. *See* call price and callable.

callable Term applying to securities that contain a provision giving the issuer the right to retire the issue before maturity, in whole or in part, at a fixed call price, on or after a specified date. A conditional or soft call exists when a company has the right to call a bond if the underlying stock trades at a price that exceeds the conversion price for a certain number of days.

call option The contractual right (not obligation) to buy a security from someone in the future at a predetermined price and time. A means of altering the risks and rewards of a portfolio.

call price The amount of money a corporation is obliged to pay upon redemption of senior securities before maturity. In the case of bonds, the price is usually expressed as a percentage of par. In the case of preferred stock, the call price is the price per share. The call price generally starts above par and is reduced periodically.

ceiling Often associated with floating-rate securities. The "floater" will change the rate it pays up to a ceiling, or cap, and can go no higher. *See* floor. So, if short rates go from 7 percent to 14 percent and your floater is capped at 10 percent, in effect, your floater has a fixed rate of 10 percent.

common stock   Securities that represent an ownership interest in a corporation. If the company had also issued preferred stock, both common and preferred have ownership rights, but the preferred normally has a prior claim on dividends, and, in the event of liquidation, on assets. Claims of both common and preferred shareholders are junior to claims of bondholders or other creditors of the company. Common shareholders assume the greater risk if the venture is unsuccessful but generally exercise the greater control and may gain the greater reward in the form of dividends and capital appreciation if the business succeeds. The terms "common stock" and "capital stock" are often used interchangeably.

conversion parity   Either the price at which common must sell for the market price of the convertible to equal its conversion value or the price at which a convertible must sell for it to equal the current market value of the shares obtainable upon conversion. Conversion is not economical unless the bond, preferred or warrant, is trading at a price close to conversion parity. If there is a premium or spread between the convertible price and conversion parity, it is generally better to sell the convertible and buy the stock rather than to convert.

conversion premium   The premium an investor pays for a convertible over its conversion value.

conversion price   The stated fixed price at which the holder of a convertible may purchase stock from the company through exercise of the conversion privilege. The conversion price is usually paid by surrendering the equivalent in par value of specified senior securities. Sometimes cash is also payable on conversion. In the case of warrants, cash alone may be required. *Example:* A $1,000 bond with a conversion price of $50 per share may be exchanged for 20 shares of common stock regardless of the market price of the common stock.

conversion privilege   An option to buy securities at a fixed price and other stipulated conditions, accomplished by the surrender of a senior convertible security such as a bond or preferred stock, plus a stipulated cash payment in some instances. A conversion privilege is similar to a warrant attached to a straight bond where the bond is usable at par in lieu of cash.

conversion ratio The number of shares of common stock for which a bond or preferred stock is exchangeable. For bonds, the ratio is usually expressed as the number of shares per preferred share.

conversion value The worth of a bond, preferred or warrant, if it were converted under the terms of the privilege and if the common stock obtained by conversion were sold at its current market price, disregarding commissions and adjustments for interest, if any. For a bond or preferred stock, the computation is: number of shares per warrant times common stock price, minus exercise price. Also known as actual, intrinsic or tangible value in the case of warrants.

convertible bond A bond, debenture or other debt instrument that may be exchanged at the option of the holder into common stock or other security in accordance with the terms of the conversion privilege. A convertible debenture is a bond secured by the credit of the issuer rather than any specific assets.

convertible preferred stock A senior equity that may be exchanged at the option of the holder into common stock or other securities, in accordance with the terms of the conversion privilege. A class of capital stock of a corporation; the dividend rate is specified and voted on by the board of directors, usually quarterly. Has preference over common stock dividends and liquidation of assets.

convertible security A convertible bond, convertible preferred stock, a bond with warrants attached or a warrant that may be exchanged for another security at the option of the holder, upon the surrender of the convertible security, or the convertible security plus cash or equivalent.

convertible stock notes Instead of paying in cash, the note pays in common stock or cash at issuer's option. Sometimes referred to as payment-in-kind security (PIKs).

convertibles with reset features Resets used as sweeteners to help sell the bonds. Allows for adjustment of coupon rate, conversion ratio and maturity date if certain events occur.

convexity (positive) Term used to describe a portfolio whose price rises more rapidly than an index in a bull market (when rates are declining) and falls more slowly in a bear market (when rates are rising) than an index. Although it technically does not apply to stocks, in stock market terms, if the Dow is up 10 percent and your stock is up 20 percent, and later the Dow falls 20 percent but your stock only falls 15 percent, your stock has shown positive convexity.

coupons Dated certificates, attached to a bond, that represent periodic interest payments. The coupons are clipped as they become due. Most new bonds are issued as registered (in the names of the owners), or book entry (in the names of the owners at the registrar, no certificate issued). Coupon clipping is fast becoming a thing of the past.

cum dividend With the dividend.

cumulative convertible preferred stock If the dividend is not paid, it accumulates in arrears and usually must be satisfied before any dividends can be paid on the common stock.

current yield The simple yield on a bond or preferred stock, figured by dividing the annual amount of interest by the current market price of the bond or preferred.

debenture An unsecured long-term certificate of debt issued by a corporation.

debenture with warrants A debenture or bond issue that has a specified number of warrants attached to each bond. Provisions are usually made for the detachability of the warrants and the transfer of debentures with or without the warrants, after a specified date.

debt security A bond, debenture or note.

default Failure to perform a contract obligation, such as the payment of a bond or note interest coupon, maintenance of working capital requirements or payment of principal via sinking fund at maturity.

delayed convertibility A conversion privilege or warrant that is not immediately exercisable and does not become exercisable until a future date.

delta (option) How sensitive an option's price is to a change in the price of the security that can be bought or sold with that option. As a general example, if the price of the security rose by one point and the option rose by one point, the current delta would be 1. If the security rose in price by one point and the option rose by one-half point, the option would have a delta of .5.

dilution The increase in the total amount of common stock issued by a corporation because of the conversion of warrants and convertibles. Under certain circumstances, the earnings per share and the net asset value per share may be affected by the dilution process. Dilution also refers to the issuing of additional stock in general.

discount The amount by which a bond may be selling below its face or par value.

discounted cash flow analysis Determining the present value of a future stream of cash flow (interest and principal) payments.

dividend yield The annualized dividend, divided by the price of the security.

due bill A contract to deliver a security "when issued" (*see* when issued) or to deliver a dividend payment on stock sold "cum dividend," used when the record date for the dividend is near.

earnings per share A company's reported earnings, after taxes, divided by the number of common shares outstanding. Adjustments are sometimes made if additional shares were issued during the period. No adjustment is generally made for potential conversion of senior securities or exercise warrants, unless earnings are reported on a "diluted" basis, or on a residual equity basis if conversion of certain securities defined as "residual equity" is assumed.

equity The difference between the market value of securities held in a margin account and the amount owed on them. The difference between the market value of securities placed as collateral with a bank and the amount owed on them. A synonym for a stock interest.

Eurodollar convertible bonds   Dollar denominated and similar to convertible bonds issued in the United States. Because the bonds are not registered with the Securities and Exchange Commission, they cannot be purchased by U.S. investors until seasoned—usually 90 days. Generally pay annually. Usually shorter maturities. Some have put feature that allows investors to sell the bond back to the company at a price above par.

excess return   The difference between the return on a portfolio and the return on a risk-free rate or benchmark.

exchangeable convertible bonds   Convertible bonds may be issued by one company and converted into stock of another company. *Example:* IBM owned block of Intel common. IBM issued a convertible bond exchangeable for Intel's common. The security had the credit obligation guaranteed by IBM but the stock potential of Intel, a growth company, in the microchip industry. The bond carried a coupon of 6.375 percent, was convertible into 26.143 shares of Intel common and was rated AAA by Standard & Poor's. When Intel's common rose to $60 in 1987, the bond's intrinsic value was $1,568.86.

exchangeable convertible preferred   Gives the company the additional option of exchanging the convertible preferred stock for convertible bonds.

ex-dividend   A stock trading without the current dividend.

exercise   To take advantage of an option to buy stock by converting a bond or preferred stock into common stock, or by surrendering a warrant with the exercise price in exchange for the optioned stock. Exercise usually takes place when the price of the stock via exercise is lower than the price of an open-market purchase. When an option is about to expire or when terms are about to change, exercise may be forced.

exercise price   Price at which the underlying stock is either bought or sold.

expiration date   The date on which an option, warrant or conversion privilege ends. If the option has value, it must be exercised on or before the expiration date; otherwise it becomes worthless.

fixed-income Income, such as bond interest or preferred stock dividends, which remains constant and does not fluctuate with the level of corporate earnings. Occasionally, a preferred stock dividend has a step-up.

flat Without accrued interest. *See* accrued interest.

floating-rate bonds An issue where the coupon rate is periodically reset based on some predetermined benchmark. Generally issued by banks or companies whose earnings are closely tied to interest rate fluctuations. This is a way to adjust how much they are paying for money they borrow.

floor The straight bond or preferred stock value without consideration of the conversion privilege. Theoretically, the floor is the approximate price at which a convertible may hold when the common stock declines to such an extent that the conversion privilege ceases to influence the market price of the convertible. Also known as the estimated investment value.

forced conversion Holders of convertible securities may be forced to convert, or sell to someone who will convert, in order to avoid a serious loss of value when there is a call for redemption, an adverse change in the conversion terms or an upcoming expiration of the privilege. Companies will usually force conversion when the underlying stock is trading well above the conversion price. This retires the bonds without a cash payment on the part of the company.

hedge A simultaneous long and short position in securities that fluctuate in unison, such as a convertible and its related common.

hypothecate To pledge negotiable securities as collateral for a loan while still retaining ownership.

immunized portfolio A portfolio intended to lock in a fixed rate of return over a specified time; for example, locking in a 9 percent return for a five-year period irrespective of interest-rate changes. Multiperiod immunization is to fund a fixed schedule of multiple future payouts.

index Various benchmarks to measure a bond portfolio's performance. Each is composed of a group of bonds that have a common quality or purpose, and are intended to represent that sector of the market that has those qualities (such as duration, type of bond, quality ratings, etc.).

intermediate term bonds   Mature in 5 to 15 years, or thereabouts, and have a duration of approximately 3 to 6.

in-the-money (option)   When the price of the stock (or contract representing a stock) that can be bought or sold with an option exceeds the option's strike price for a call option, or is below the option's strike price for a put option. *See* strike price.

investment value   The price at which a convertible bond would sell as a straight bond relative to other bonds of the same yield, maturity and quality.

junkyard dogs   Investors who enjoy hunting the high-risk bond market for values others might have overlooked.

ladder portfolio   A portfolio made up of securities that mature in equal amounts each year from, for example, 1 to 20 years.

libor   A very short maturity (90-day) benchmark against which many securities are priced and repriced at different times ("It floats off LIBOR."). Stands for London Interbank Offered Rate, which is the price at which banks loan to each other.

long-term bonds   Generally have maturities of 15 years or more, and a duration of 6 or more.

market premium over conversion value   The extra price investors are willing to pay for a convertible security in excess of its conversion or intrinsic value. The premium is usually paid for an additional safety factor, extra yield, leverage potential or any combination of these. The premium is computed as follows: market price of convertible minus conversion value. Expressed as a percentage: market price of convertible less conversion value, divided by conversion value × 100. The percentage premium represents the percentage rise needed in the common stock for the convertible to be worth its current market price.

maturity   A fixed date when the face amount of a bond becomes due and payable.

negative convexity   If your bond portfolio rises in price more slowly in a bull market than it declines in price in a bear market, it is said to have negative convexity.

out-of-the-money (options)   When the price of a stock (or contract representing a stock) that can be bought or sold with an option is below the strike price for a call option, and above the strike price for a put option, it is said to be out-of-the-money.

par   The face value of a security. In the case of preferred shares and bonds, par signifies the dollar value upon which dividends on preferred stocks and interest on bonds are figured. The issue of a 5 percent bond promises to pay that percentage of the bond's par value annually. Par value of a bond is 100.

parity   When the price of a convertible security is exactly equivalent to the value of the common stock obtainable upon immediate conversion, the two issues are said to be selling at a parity. *See* conversion parity.

PIK (payment-in-kind)   A financing technique whereby they give you more of the same to pay the interest.

plus cash   Descriptive of a convertible bond or convertible preferred stock that requires an additional cash payment upon conversion. *See* conversion value.

premium over conversion value   *See* market premium over conversion value.

price to book value   Book value is a theoretical value of a company's tangible assets, assuming all debt was paid off. It represents what you are buying when you invest in a stock.

put option   The contractual right (not obligation) to sell a security to someone in the future at a predetermined price and time.

puttable bond   A bond that carries the right to sell, or put, the bond back to the issuer.

quick breakeven calculation   Percent premium divided by yield differential. Sometimes referred to as payback period.

registered bond   A bond issued in the name of the holder. Interest is paid by check if there are no coupons, in which case the bond is said to be fully registered, or registered as to principal and interest. Most recent issues of convertible bonds are fully registered.

senior securities   Bonds or preferred stocks that are entitled to a prior claim over the common stock in the distribution of current earnings or interest, or to assets in case of liquidation.

strike price   In options, the agreed-upon price at which the underlying security may be bought or sold.

stripped bonds   Bonds, originally issued with warrants, that trade without warrants, or ex-warrants.

synthetic convertibles   Combining a fixed-income security with an equity security. Some refer to the process as "gluing up" pieces in proper amounts; for example, buying a bond and some warrants, or some call options. The correct proportion of warrants or call options to bonds could be determined by dividing the exercise price into \$1,000. If the warrants are exercisable at \$50, the number that should be held is 20 (\$100 ÷ \$50 = 20).

total return   The combination of coupon income received and change in price of the security over a period of time.

unit option valuation   An analysis of conversion privileges and warrants to determine the cost of an option on one share of common, tangible value, option amount and percent, and leverage factors.

units   A package of securities issued and traded in units.

warrants   A negotiable security issued by a company representing an option to buy its unissued common stock on specified terms with regard to the number of shares, the price to be paid on exercise of the privilege, and the time element.

when issued   A short form of "when, as, and if issued." The term indicates a conditional transaction in a security authorized for issuance but not as yet actually issued. All "when issued" transactions are on an "if" basis, to be settled if and when the actual security is issued and the Exchange or National Association of Securities Dealers rules that the transactions are to be settled.

with warrants   Bonds quoted "ww," with warrants, indicating that warrants are attached.

workout   The process of restructuring and recapitalizing a company to restore its financial health. WARTs are companies that undergo these workout acquisitions, restructuring and turnarounds. Just who will emerge the WART king has yet to be determined.

yield   Also known as return. The dividends or interest paid annually by a company on a security, expressed as a percentage of the current price—or, in some cases, of the price originally paid for the security.

yield differential   The difference between the current yield of the convertible security and the current yield of the underlying common stock.

yield to maturity   The effective yield of a bond taking into account the premium or discount from par, the coupon and the remaining time to maturity when the issue is expected to be redeemed at par.

zero-coupon convertibles (LYONs)   Liquid-Yield Option Notes combine zeros with stock. Created by Merrill Lynch in 1982, LYONs are corporate zero-coupon bonds with the right to convert to the underlying common stock put feature.

INDEX